SHINEDOWN A

Music transcriptions by Pete Billmann, Addi Booth and David Stocker

ISBN 978-1-4584-9734-5

7777 W. BLUEMOUND RD. P.O. BOX 13819 MILWAUKEE, WI 53213

In Australia Contact:
Hal Leonard Australia Pty. Ltd.
4 Lentara Court
Cheltenham, Victoria, 3192 Australia
Email: ausadmin@halleonard.com.au

Visit Hal Leonard Online at
www.halleonard.com

Adrenaline

Words and Music by Brent Smith and Dave Bassett

Drop D tuning, down 1/2 step:
(low to high) Db-Ab-Db-Gb-Bb-Eb

Intro
Moderately fast ♩ = 160

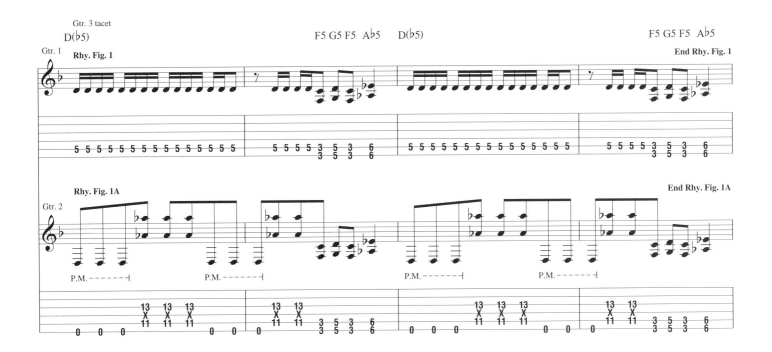

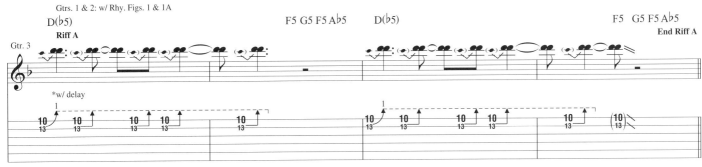

*Set for quarter-note regeneration w/ 1 repeat.

Verse

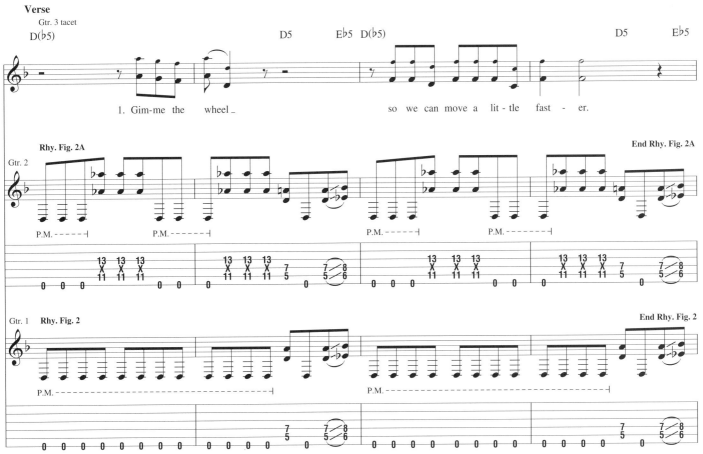

1. Gim-me the wheel _ so we can move a lit-tle fast - er.

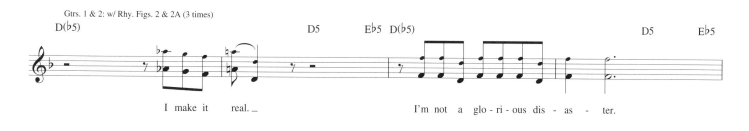

I make it real.___   I'm not a glo-ri-ous dis-as-ter.

What part of liv-ing says you got-ta die?_____   I plan on burn-in' through an-oth-er nine lives.

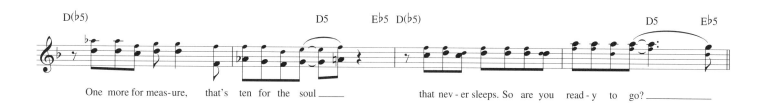

One more for meas-ure,   that's ten for the soul_____   that nev-er sleeps. So are you read-y to go?_____

𝄋 Chorus

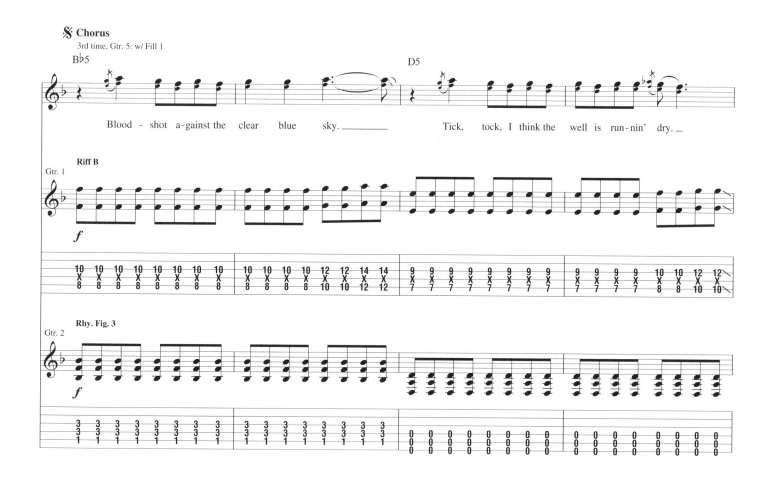

Blood-shot a-gainst the clear blue sky._____   Tick, tock, I think the well is run-nin' dry.___

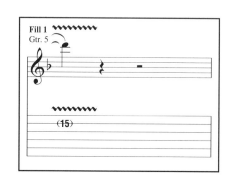

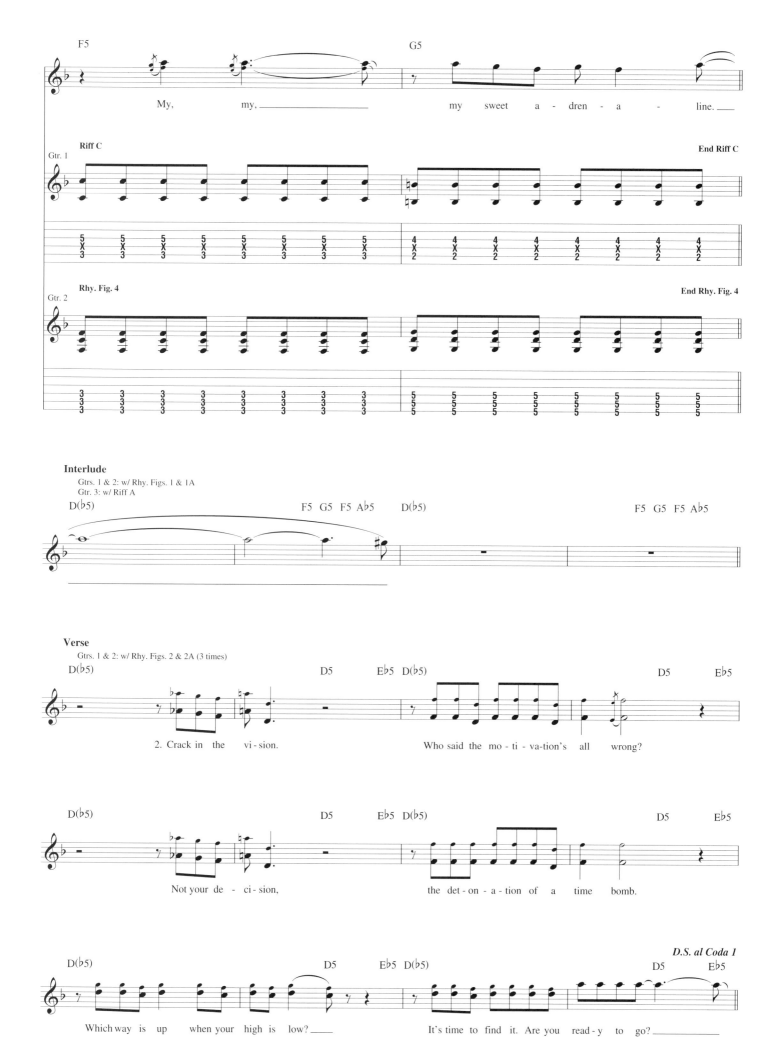

My, my, _____ my sweet a - dren - a - line. ___

Riff C

Gtr. 1

End Riff C

Rhy. Fig. 4

Gtr. 2

End Rhy. Fig. 4

Interlude

Gtrs. 1 & 2: w/ Rhy. Figs. 1 & 1A
Gtr. 3: w/ Riff A

D(♭5)   F5 G5 F5 A♭5   D(♭5)   F5 G5 F5 A♭5

Verse

Gtrs. 1 & 2: w/ Rhy. Figs. 2 & 2A (3 times)

D(♭5)   D5   E♭5 D(♭5)   D5   E♭5

2. Crack in the vi - sion.   Who said the mo - ti - va-tion's all wrong?

D(♭5)   D5   E♭5 D(♭5)   D5   E♭5

Not your de - ci-sion,   the det - on - a - tion of a time bomb.

D.S. al Coda 1

D(♭5)   D5   E♭5 D(♭5)   D5   E♭5

Which way is up   when your high is low? ___   It's time to find it. Are you read - y to go? _____

Coda 1

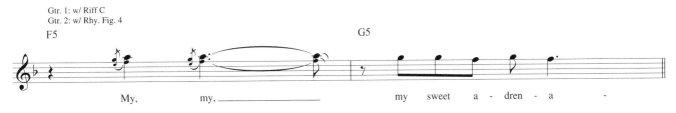

My, my, _____ my sweet a - dren - a -

Interlude

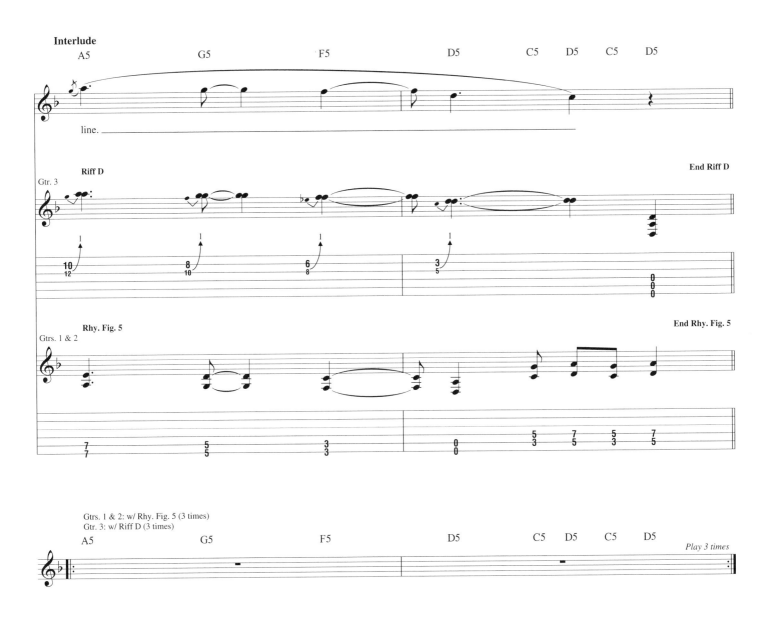

line. _____

Bridge

My, my, I just ___ can't lie. ___ It's the speed and the sound that I'm dy - in' to try. ___

Gtr. 1

Gtr. 2

Guitar Solo

Gtr. 1: w/ Riff B
Gtr. 2: w/ Rhy. Fig. 3

Bb5

*Gtr. 4 (dist.)

*Doubled throughout

D5

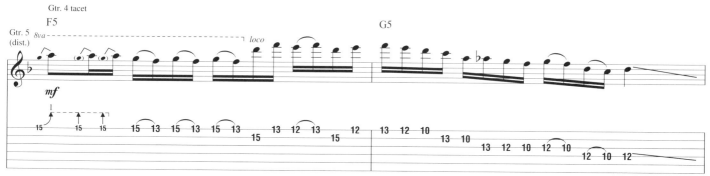

Gtr. 4 tacet

F5   G5

Gtr. 5

(dist.)

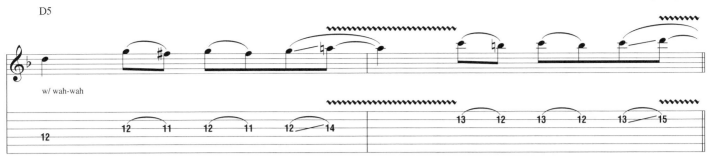

w/ wah-wah

⊕ Coda 2

Bkgd. Voc.: w/ Voc. Fig. 1
Gtr. 1: w/ Riff B (last 4 meas.)
Gtr. 2: w/ Rhy. Fig. 3 (last 4 meas.)

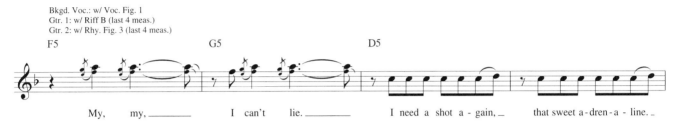

My,   my, _____   I can't   lie. _____   I need a shot a - gain, _____   that sweet a - dren - a - line. _____

Gtr. 1: w/ Riff C
Gtr. 2: w/ Rhy. Fig. 4

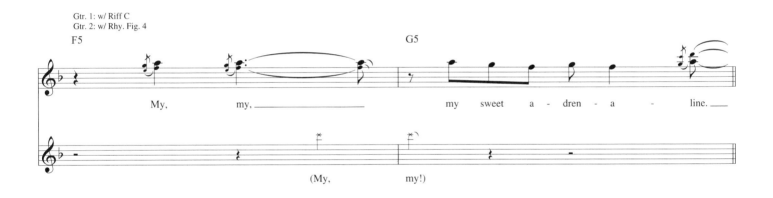

My,   my, _____   my sweet a - dren - a - line. _____

(My,   my!)

Outro

Gtrs. 1 & 2: w/ Rhy. Figs. 1 & 1A (2 times)
Gtr. 3: w/ Riff A (2 times)

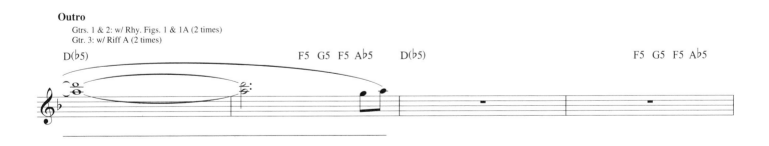

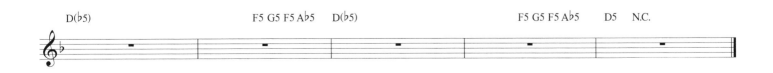

Bully

Words and Music by Brent Smith, Dave Bassett and Zachary Myers

Drop D tuning, down 1/2 step:
(low to high) Db-Ab-Db-Gb-Bb-Eb

Intro
Moderately ♩ = 155
N.C.

Hey!

Rhy. Fig. 1
*Gtr. 1 (dist.)

End Rhy. Fig. 1

mf

*Doubled throughout

Half-time feel
**D5

Hey!

Riff A

End Riff A

f

***w/ octaver

1/2   1   1/2   1

0   3   0   5   (5)   3   0   3   0   5   0   3   0   5   (5)   3   0   3   0   5

**Chord symbols reflect basic harmony.
***Set for 2 octaves above.

Verse
Gtr. 1 tacet
D5

1. It's eight a. m., ____ this hell I'm in. ____

Rhy. Fig. 2
†Gtr. 2 (slight dist.)

mf

3   3
2   2
0   0

†Doubled throughout   ††w/ echo set for half-note regeneration w/ 1 repeat.   †††As before

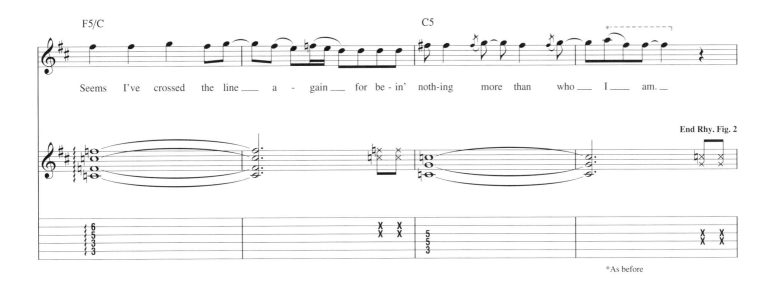

Seems I've crossed the line ___ a - gain ___ for be-in' noth-ing more than who ___ I ___ am.

End Rhy. Fig. 2

*As before

Gtr. 2: w/ Rhy. Fig. 2 (1st 4 meas.)

So break my bones ___ and throw your stones. ___

**As before   ***As before

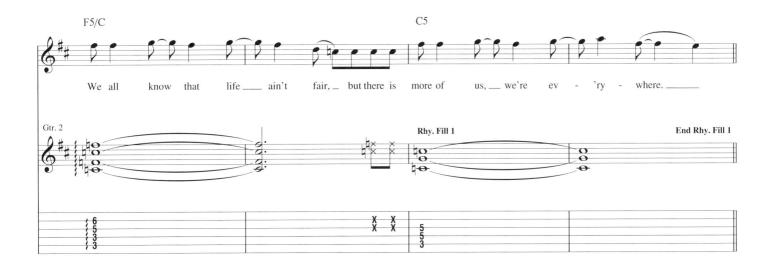

We all know that life ___ ain't fair, ___ but there is more of us, ___ we're ev - 'ry - where. ___

Gtr. 2   Rhy. Fill 1   End Rhy. Fill 1

Pre-Chorus

Gtr. 2 tacet   Gtr. 1: w/ Rhy. Fig. 1

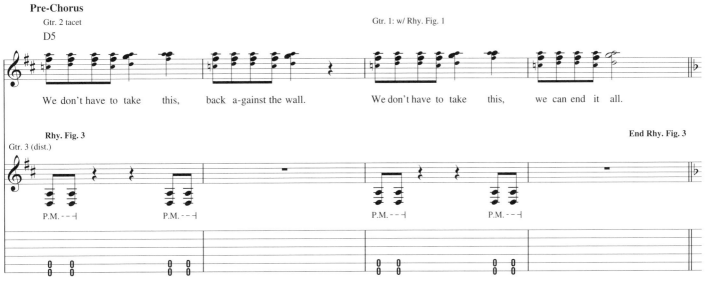

We don't have to take this, back a-gainst the wall. We don't have to take this, we can end it all.

Rhy. Fig. 3   End Rhy. Fig. 3

Gtr. 3 (dist.)

P.M. ---| P.M. ---| P.M. ---| P.M. ---|

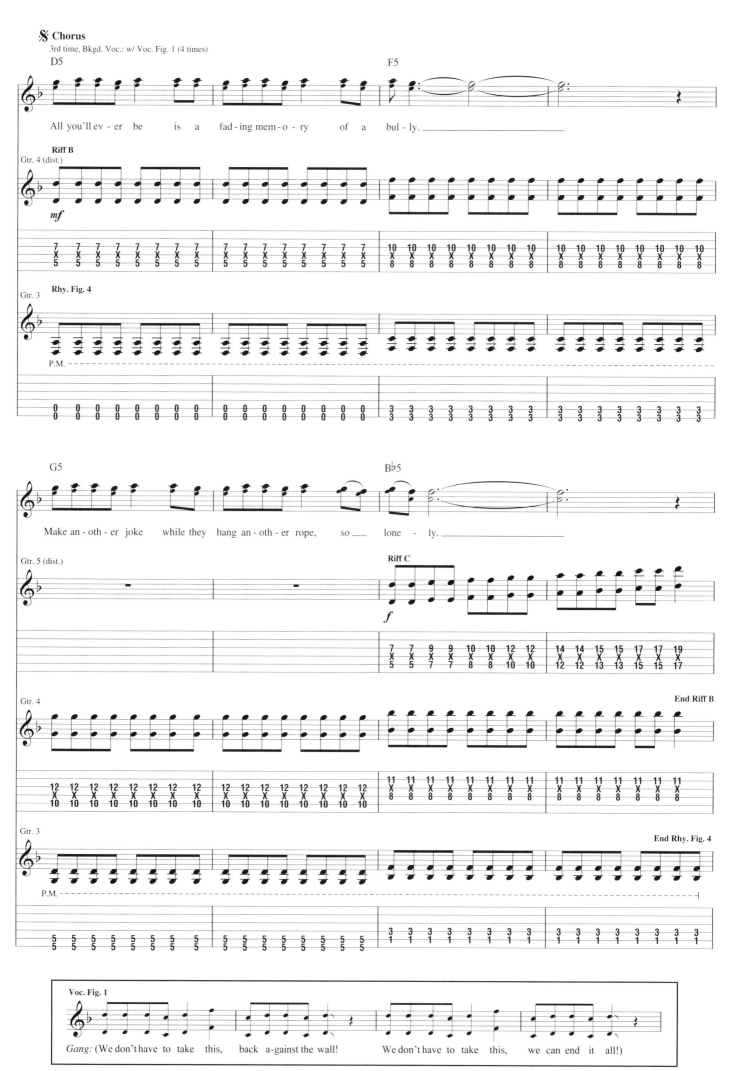

Pitch: A

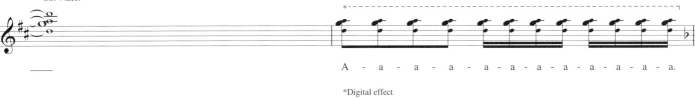

Gtr. 1: w/ Rhy. Fig. 1
Gtr. 4 tacet

A - a - a - a - a - a - a - a - a - a - a - a.

*Digital effect

⊕ Coda 1

Guitar Solo

Gtr. 4 tacet

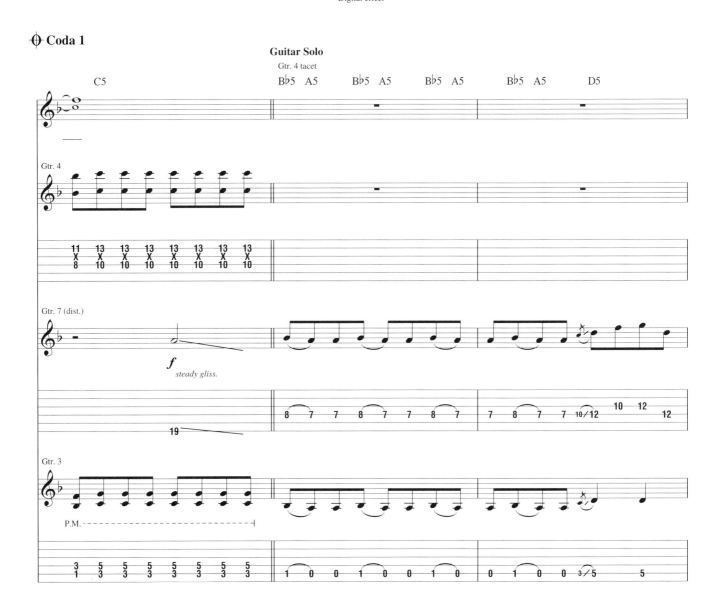

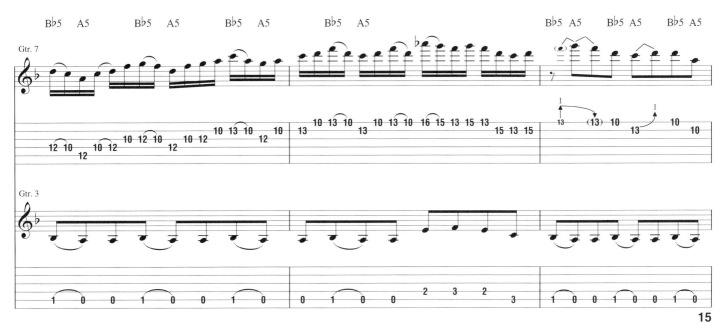

Bridge

Gtr. 1: w/ Riff A
Gtr. 3 tacet

Gtr. 7 tacet

D5

It's eight a. m., ___ the hell ___ I'm in. ___

(Ah, ___ ah, ___

Gtr. 7

steady gliss.

Gtr. 8 (dist.)

mp

(cont. on upper staff)

Chorus
Gtr. 3: w/ Rhy. Fig. 4 (1 3/4 times)
Gtr. 4: w/ Riff B (1 3/4 times)

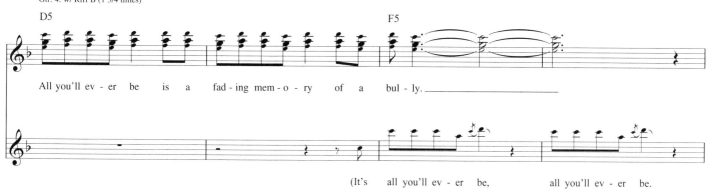

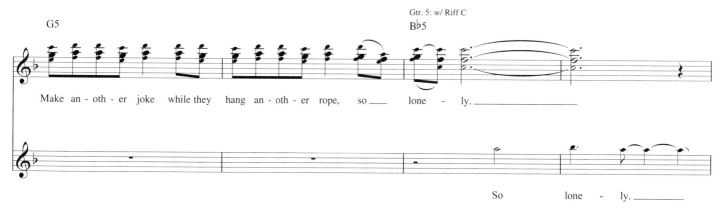

18

Amaryllis

Words and Music by Brent Smith and Dave Bassett

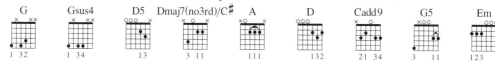

Drop D tuning, down 1/2 step:
(low to high) Db-Ab-Db-Gb-Bb-Eb

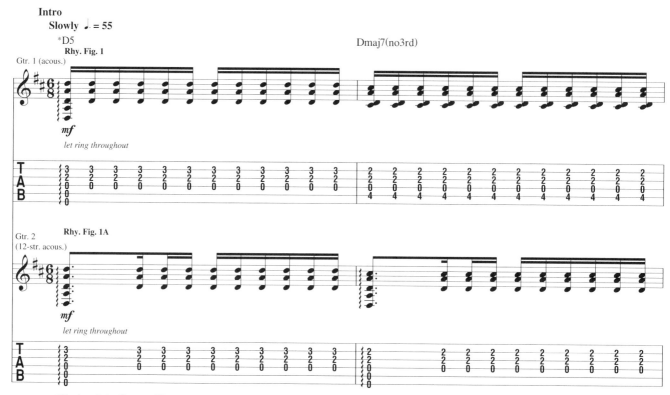

*Chord symbols reflect overall harmony.

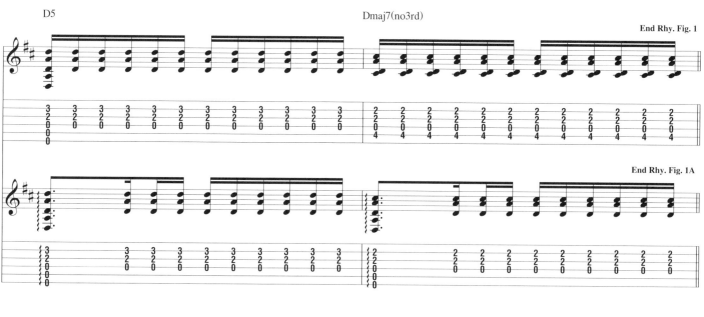

Verse

1. In __ a __ while __ now, I will feel __ bet-ter. I'll face the weath-er be - fore me. __

*Composite arrangement

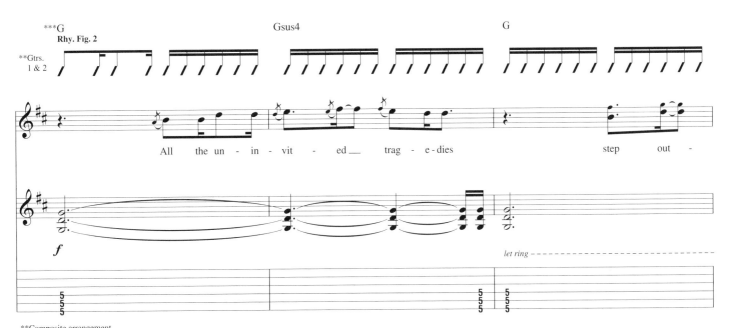

**Composite arrangement
***See top of first page of song for chord diagrams pertaining to rhythm slashes.

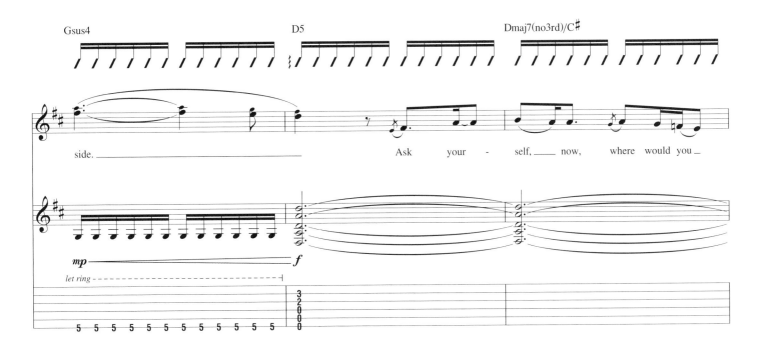

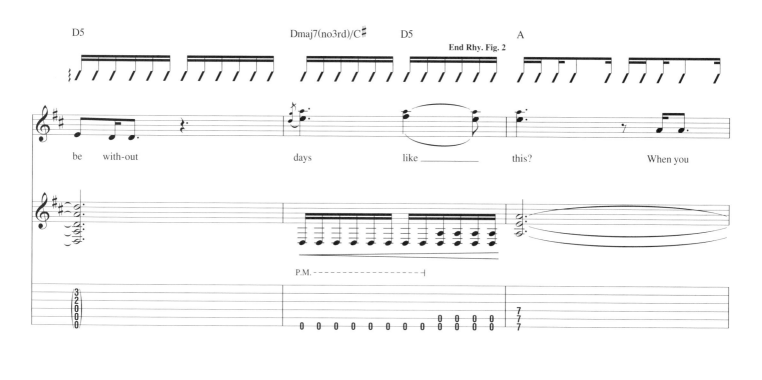

be with-out ... days like _____ this? When you

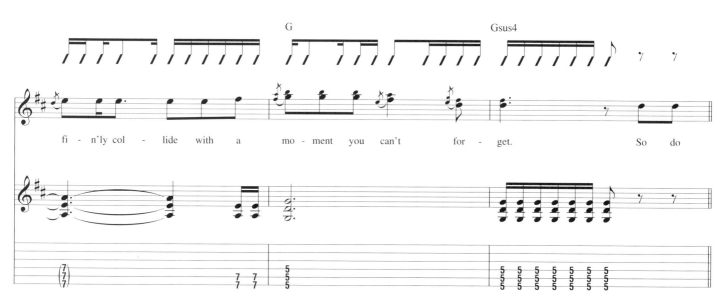

fi - n'ly col - lide with a mo - ment you can't for - get. So do

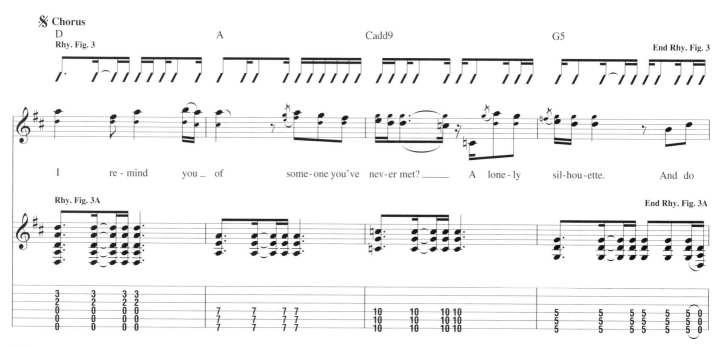

𝄋 **Chorus**

I re - mind you _ of some-one you've nev-er met? _____ A lone - ly sil-hou-ette. And do

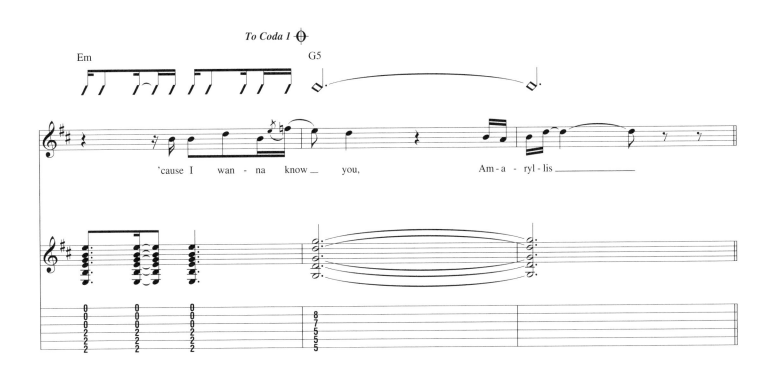

Interlude

Verse

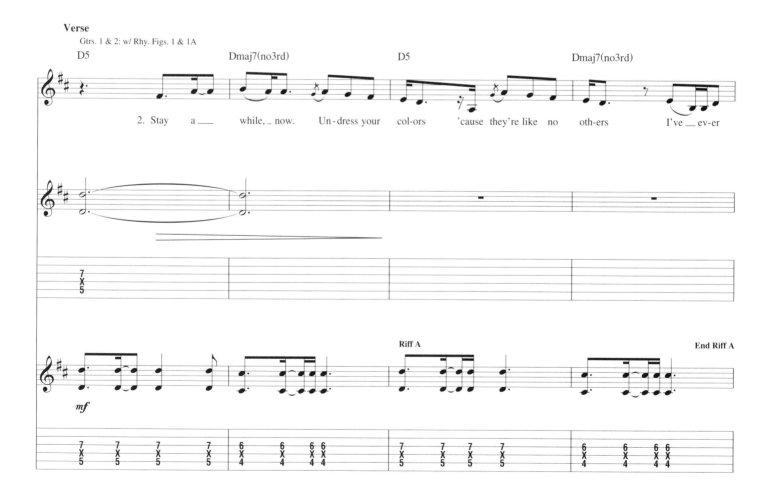

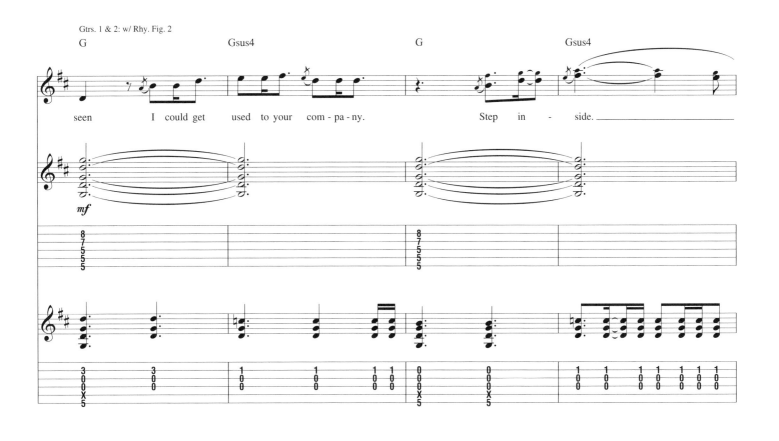

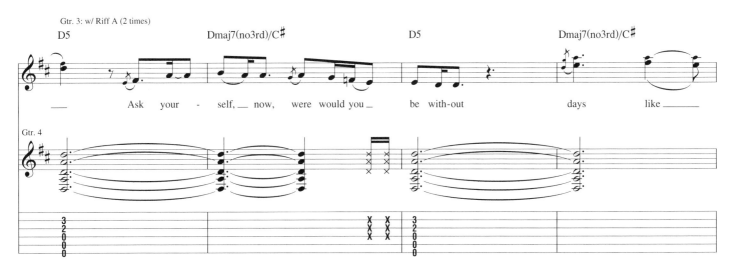

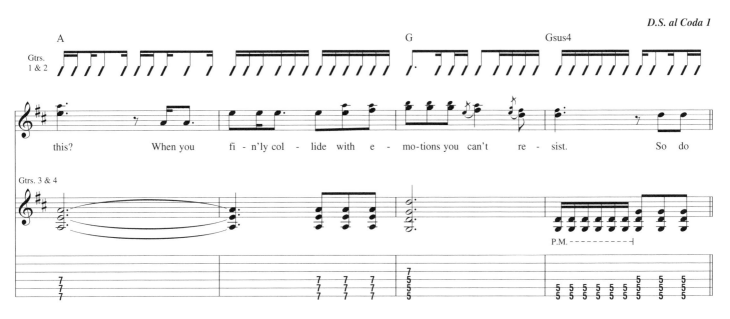

Coda 1

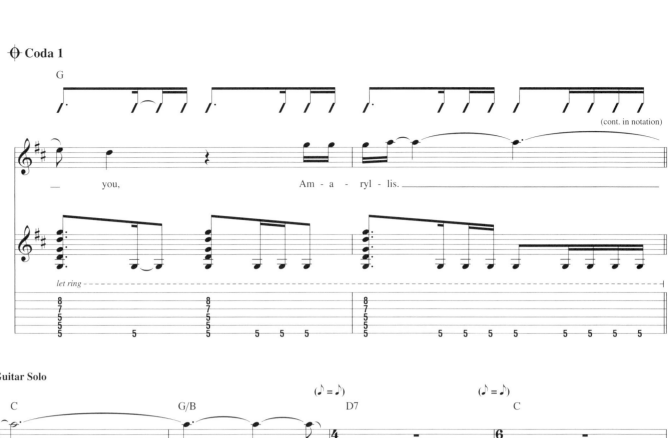

you, Am - a - ryl - lis. _____ (cont. in notation)

Guitar Solo

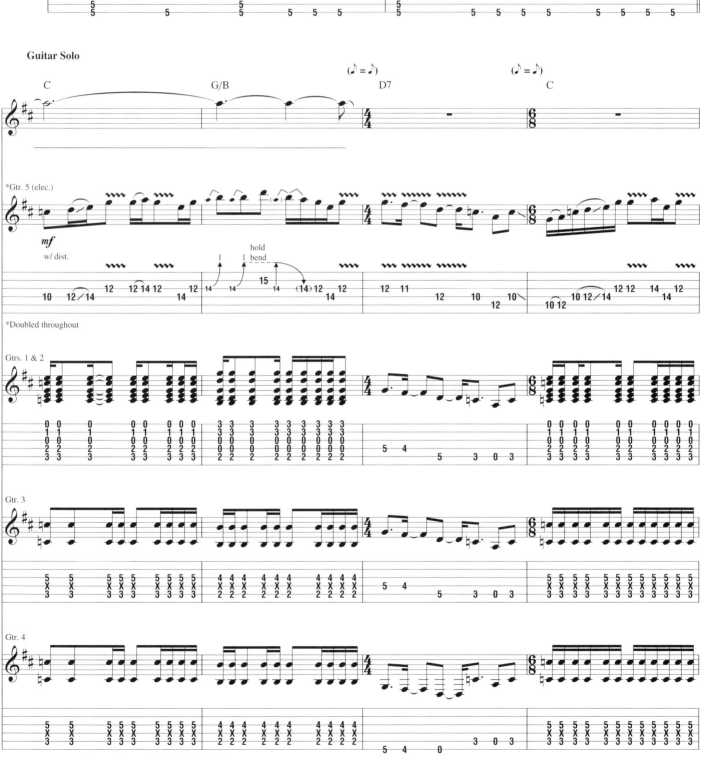

*Doubled throughout

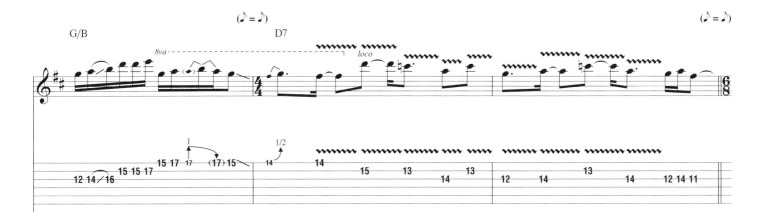

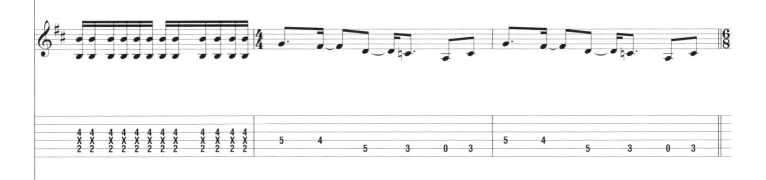

Interlude

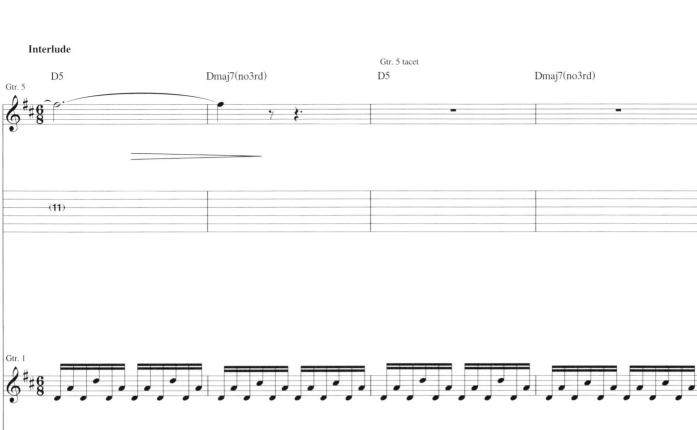

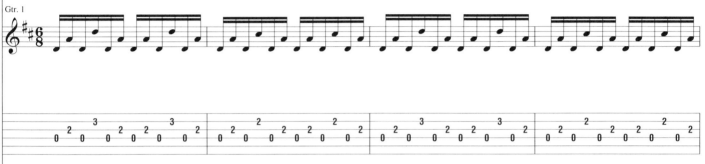

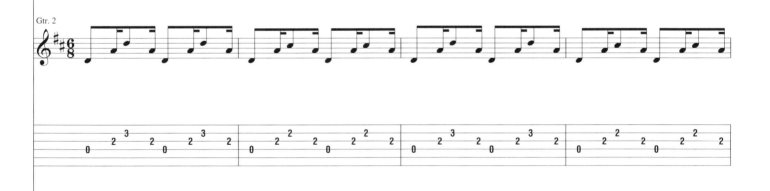

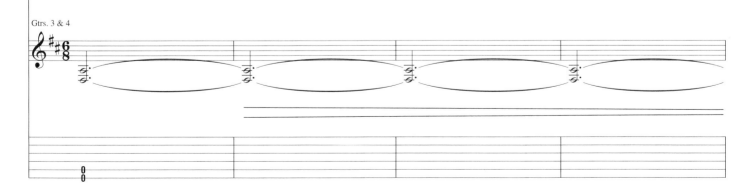

Unity

Words and Music by Brent Smith, Dave Bassett and Eric Bass

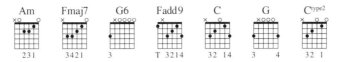

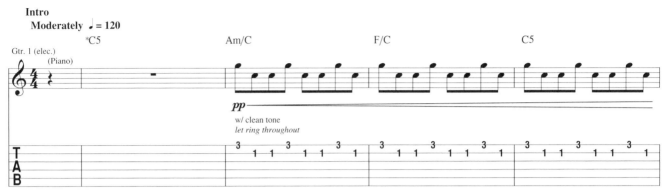

Gtr. 3: Drop D tuning, down 1 step:
(low to high) C-G-C-F-A-D

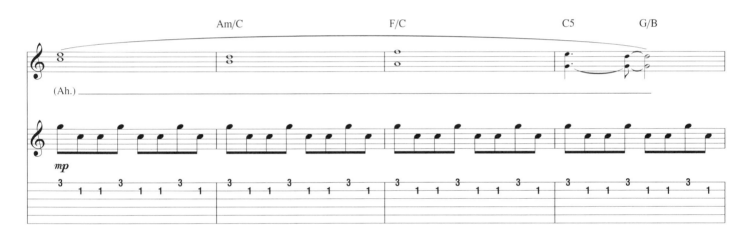

*Chord symbols reflect overall harmony.

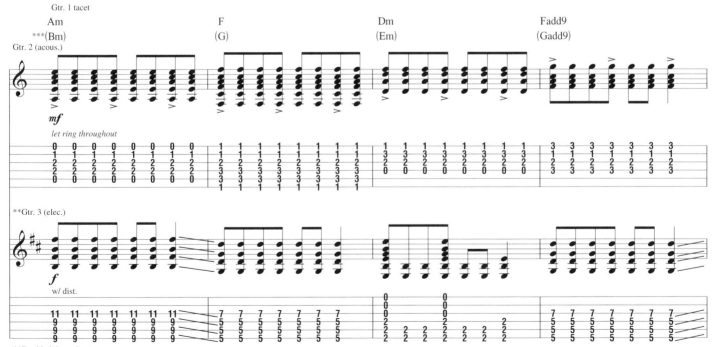

**Doubled throughout

***Symbols in parentheses represent chord names respective to detuned guitar.
Symbols above reflect actual sounding chords.

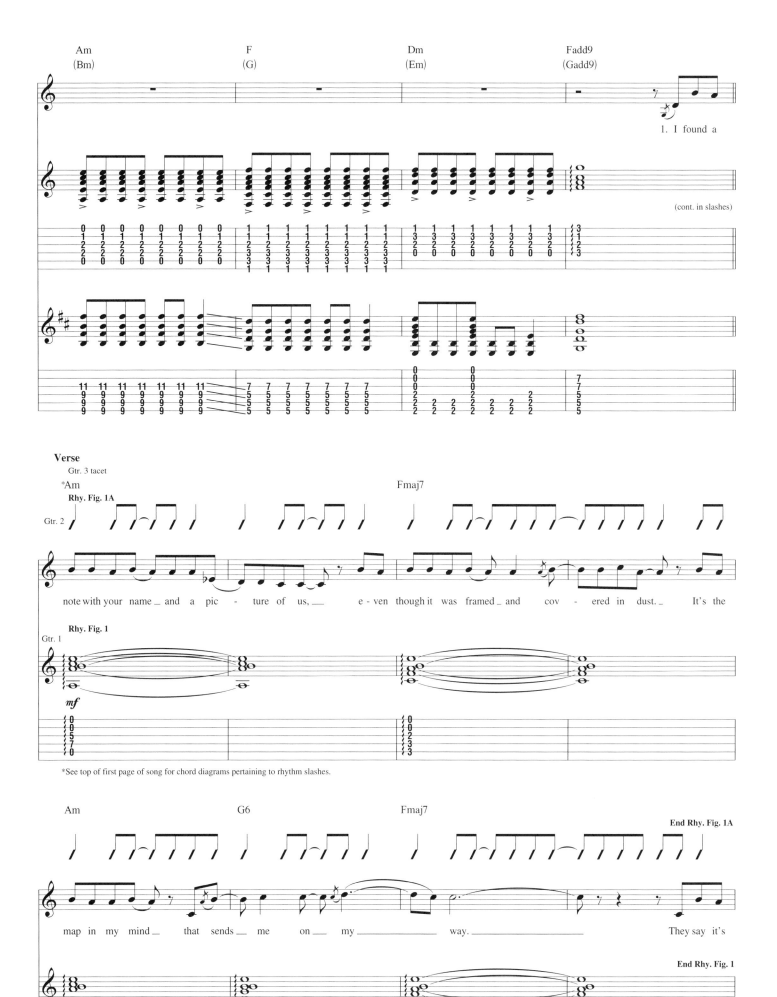

*See top of first page of song for chord diagrams pertaining to rhythm slashes.

Gtrs. 1 & 2: w/ Rhy. Figs. 1 & 1A

nev - er too late __ to stop be - ing a - fraid.   And there is   no one else here, __ so   why __ should I wait?   And in the

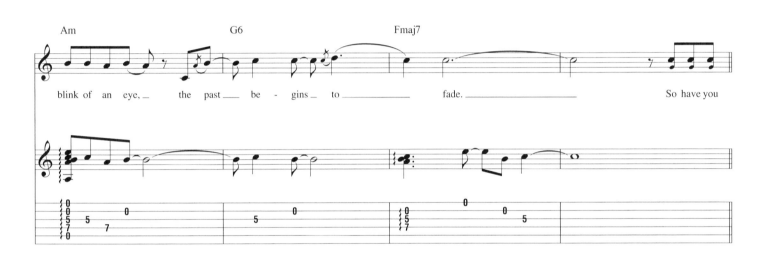

blink of an eye, __ the past __ be - gins __ to __ fade. _____   So have you

Pre-Chorus

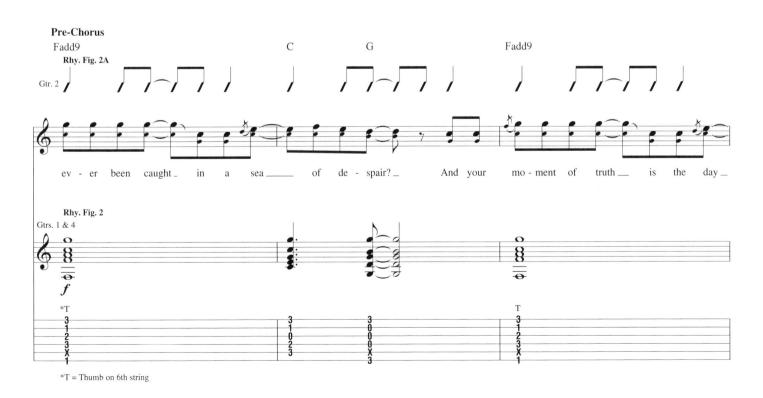

ev - er been caught __ in a sea __ of de - spair? __   And your   mo - ment of truth __ is the day __

*T = Thumb on 6th string

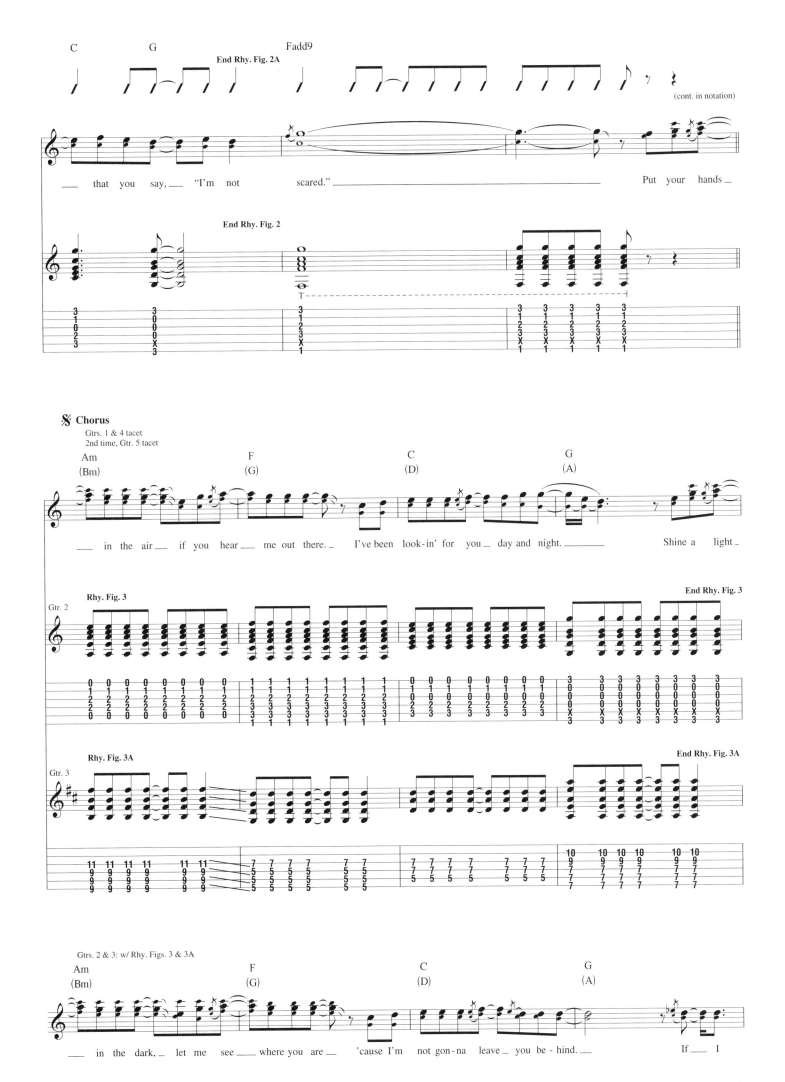

that you say, "I'm not scared." Put your hands

Put your hands

% Chorus
Gtrs. 1 & 4 tacet
2nd time, Gtr. 5 tacet

in the air if you hear me out there. I've been look-in' for you day and night. Shine a light

in the dark, let me see where you are 'cause I'm not gon-na leave you be-hind. If I

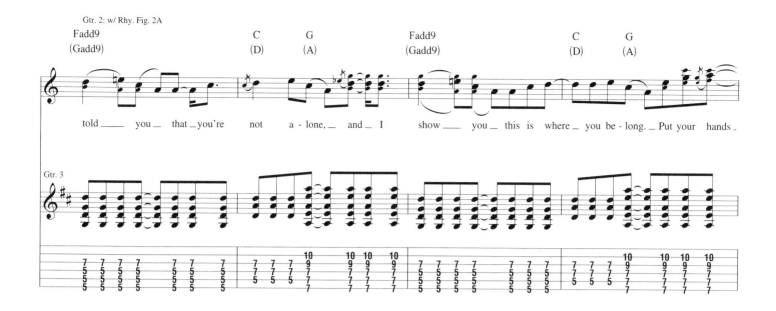

told ___ you ___ that ___ you're   not   a - lone, ___   and ___ I   show ___ you ___ this is   where ___ you be - long. ___ Put your   hands ___

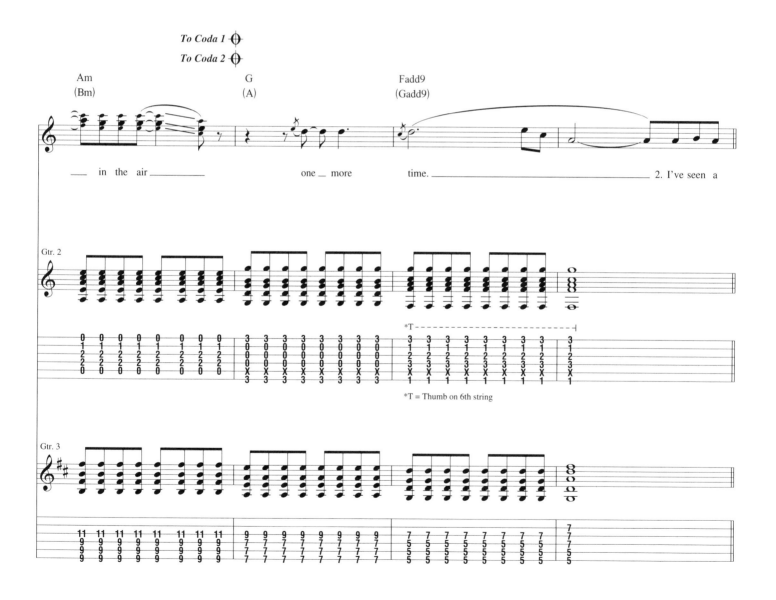

___ in the air ___   one ___ more   time. ___   2. I've seen a

*T = Thumb on 6th string

Verse

Gtrs. 1 & 2: w/ Rhy. Figs. 1 & 1A
Gtr. 3 tacet

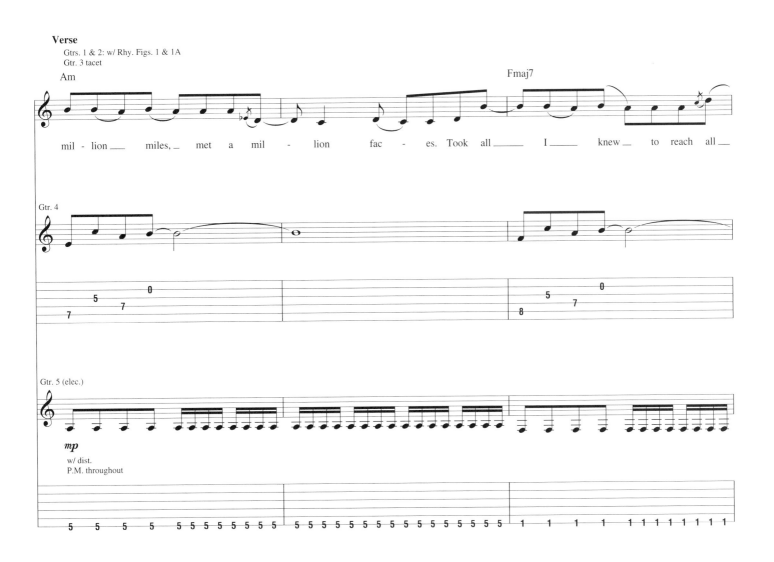

mil - lion ___ miles, ___ met a mil - lion fac - es. Took all ___ I ___ knew ___ to reach all ___

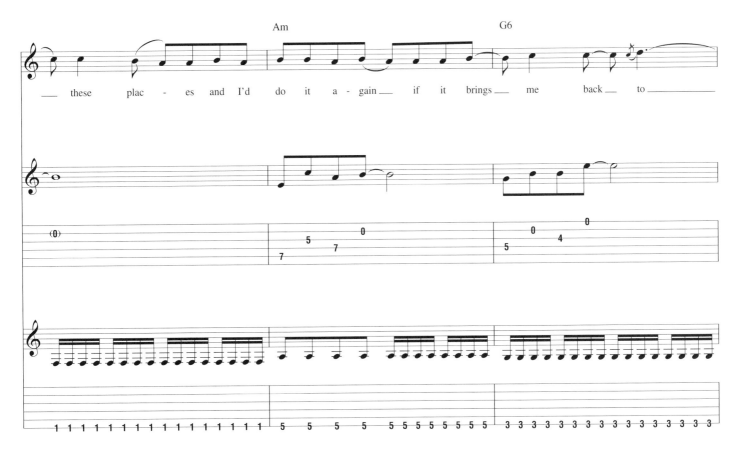

___ these plac - es and I'd do it a - gain ___ if it brings ___ me back ___ to ___

Fmaj7

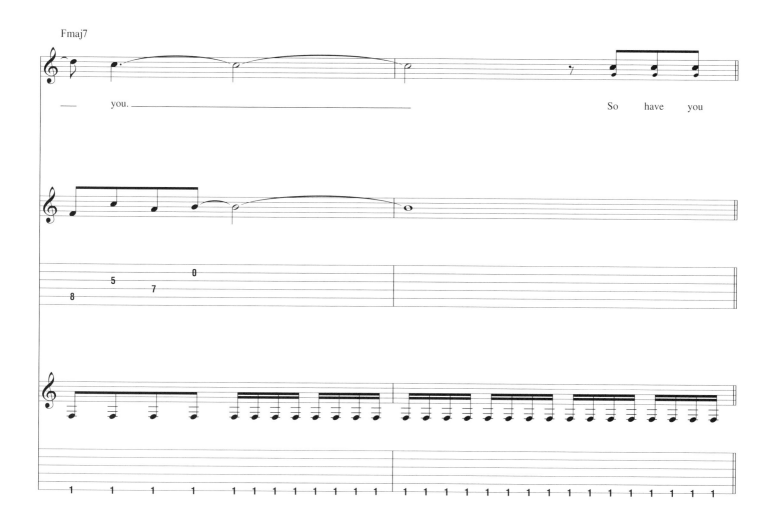

you. So have you

Pre-Chorus

Gtrs. 1 & 4: w/ Rhy. Fig. 2
Gtr. 2: w/ Rhy. Fig. 2A

Fadd9   C   G   Fadd9   C   G

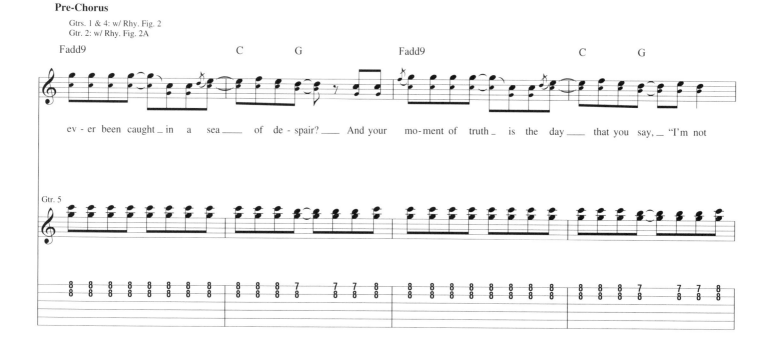

ev - er been caught _ in a sea ___ of de - spair? ___ And your mo - ment of truth _ is the day ___ that you say, _ "I'm not

Gtr. 5

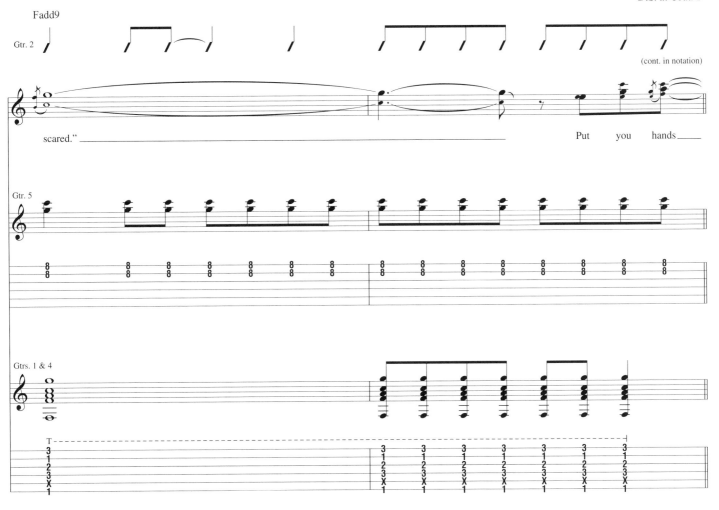

⊕ Coda 1

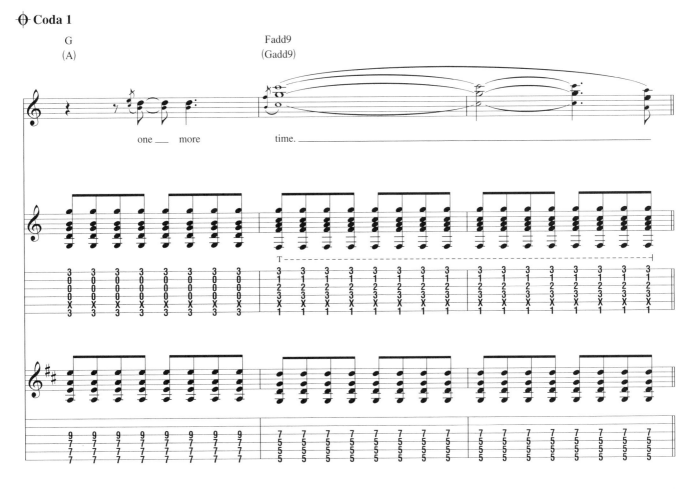

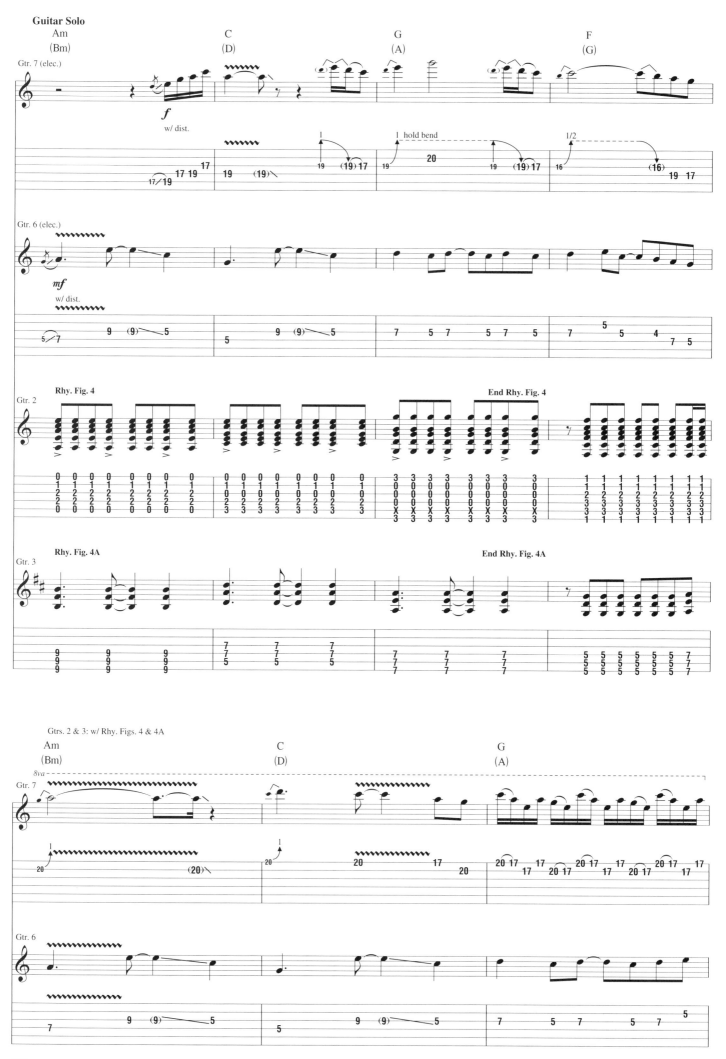

Interlude

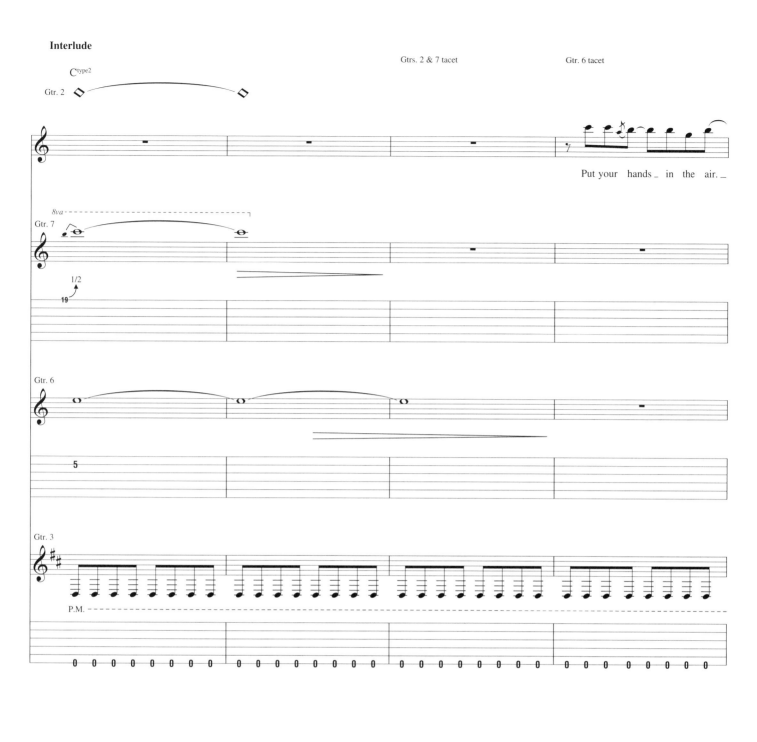

Put your hands _ in the air. _

D.S. al Coda 2

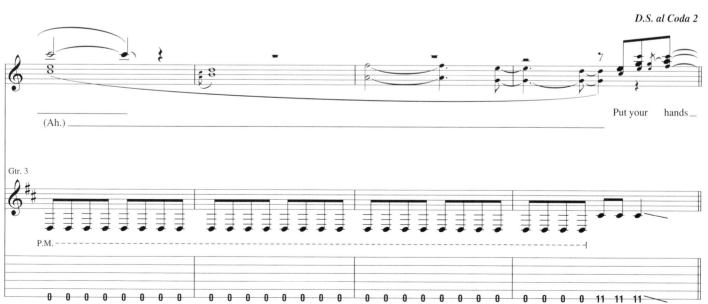

(Ah.) _____

Put your hands _

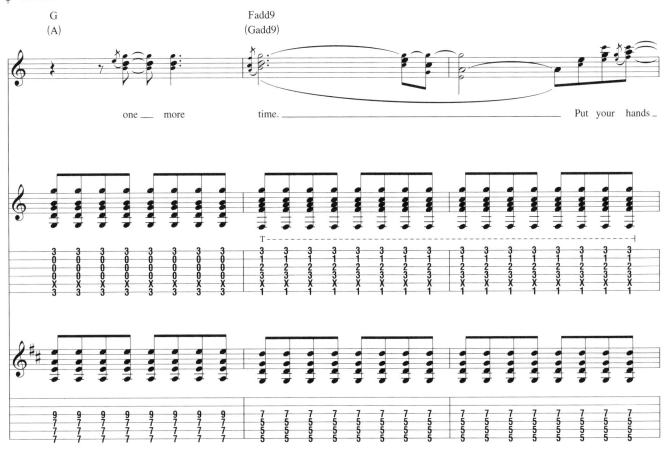

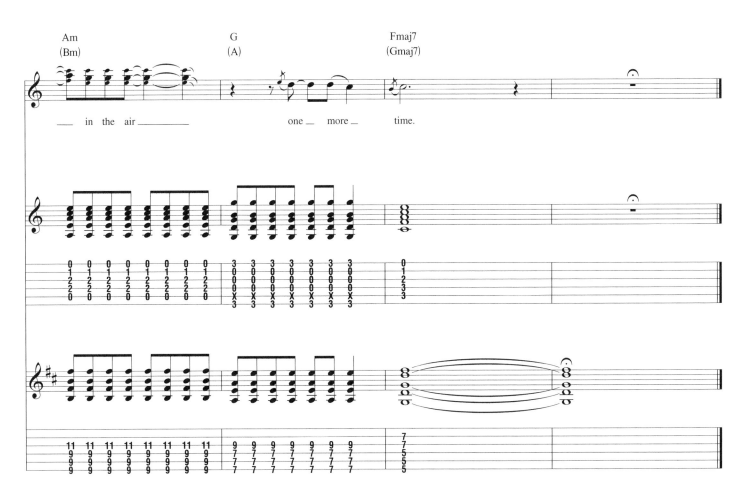

Enemies

Words and Music by Brent Smith, Dave Bassett and Eric Bass

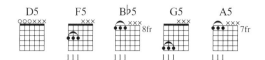

Drop D tuning, down 1 step:
(low to high) C-G-C-F-A-D

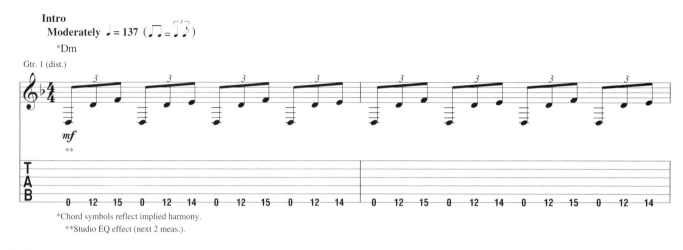

*Chord symbols reflect implied harmony.
**Studio EQ effect (next 2 meas.).

***Doubled throughout

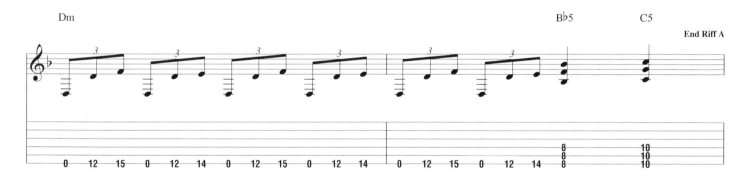

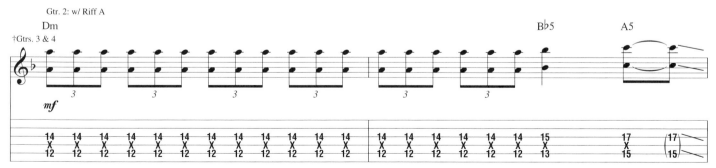

†Gtr. 3 (dist.) w/ octaver set for one octave above; Gtr. 4 (dist.)

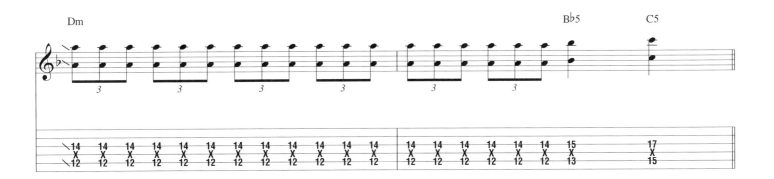

Verse

1. Lis - ten up, there's not a mo - ment to spare. ___ It's quite a
2. You start - ed some - thing that you just could - n't stop. ___ You turn the

*w/ DigiTech Whammy pedal

*Set for 2 octaves above.

Gtrs. 2 & 3: w/ Riffs B & B1 (3 times)

drop from the top, so how you feel - in' down there? ___ It's a cold, cru - el,
ones that you love in - to the an - gri - est mob. ___ And their one, last ___

harsh, re - al - i - ty, caught, stuck, here with your en - e - mies.
wish is that you pay for it. And there's no way you're get - ting out of this.

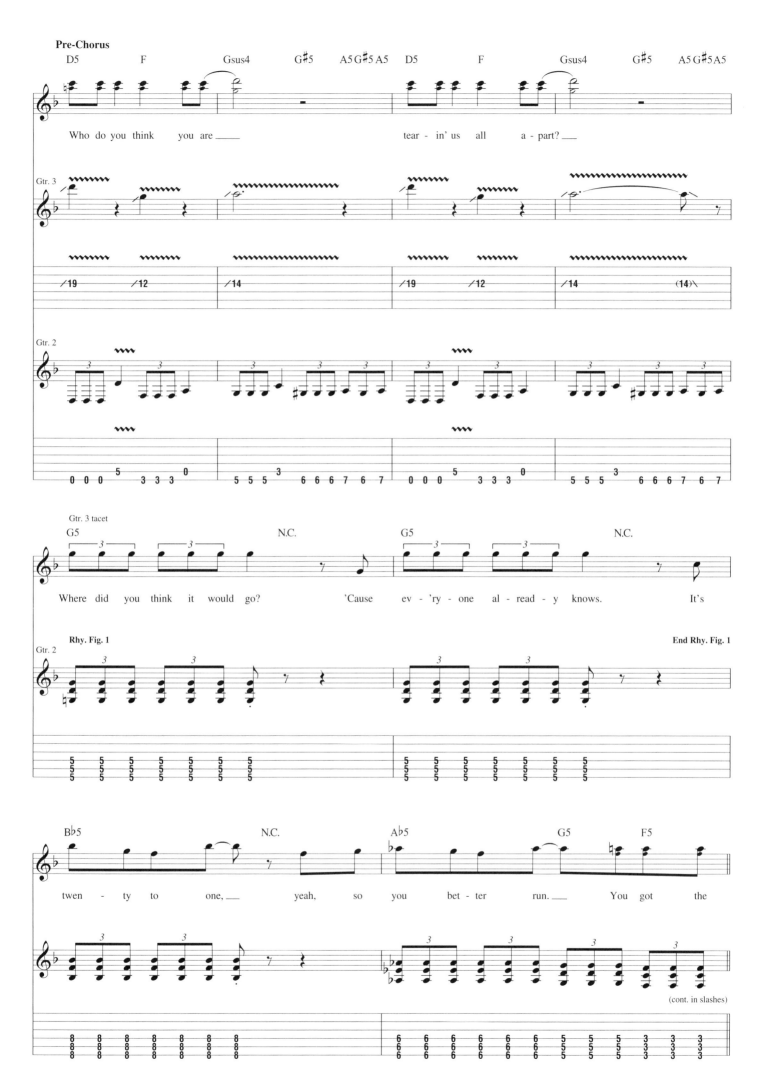

% Chorus

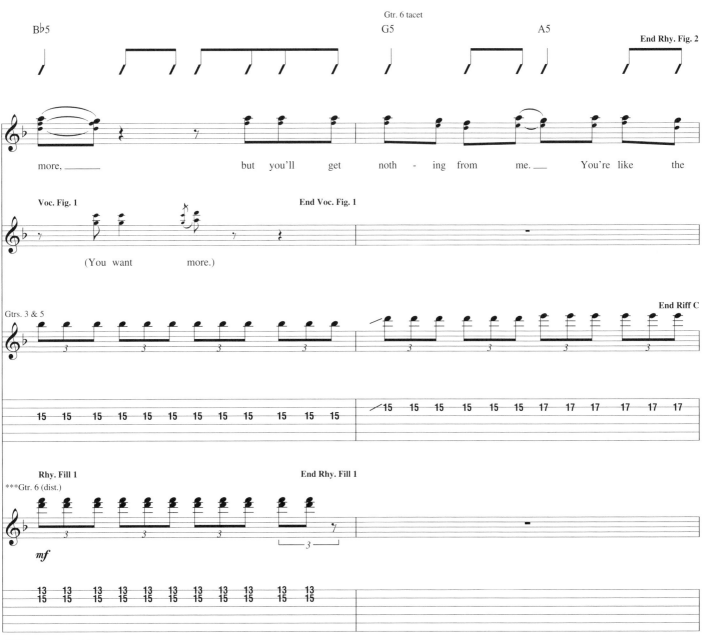

*Gtr. 3, Whammy pedal off; Gtr. 5, organ arr. for gtr.

**See top of first page of song for chord diagrams pertaining to rhythm slashes.

***Two gtrs. arr. for one.

1st & 2nd times, Gtr. 2: w/ Rhy. Fig. 2
1st & 2nd times, Gts. 3 & 5: w/ Riff C
3rd time, Gtr. 2: w/ Rhy. Fig. 2 (3 times)
3rd time, Gtrs. 3 & 5: w/ Riff C (3 times)

bur - den we bear._____ You're all the hate that we share._____ You want

Bkgd. Voc.: w/ Voc. Fig. 1
Gtr. 6: w/ Rhy. Fill 1

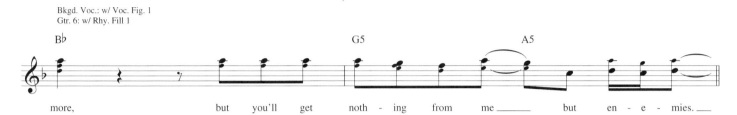

more, but you'll get noth - ing from me _____ but en - e - mies._____

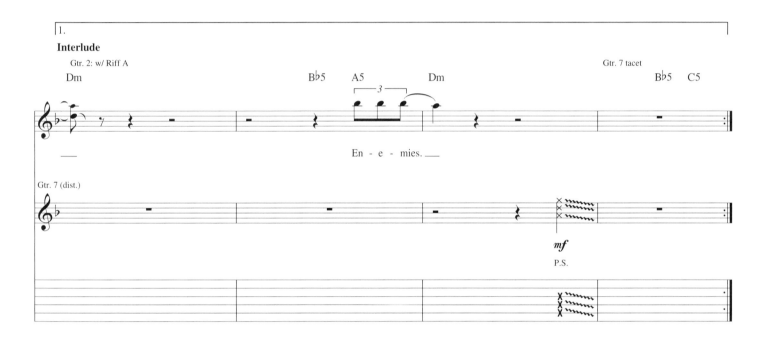

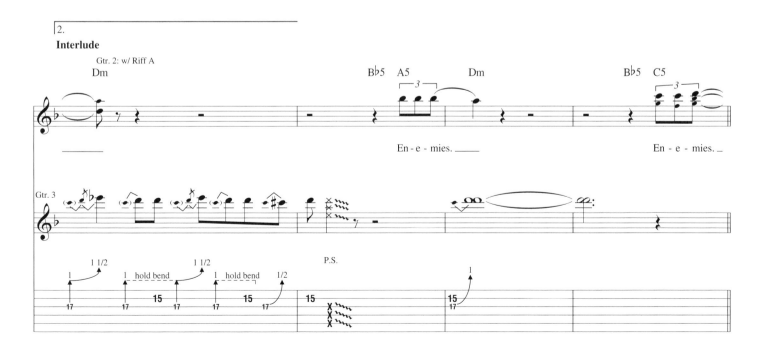

Interlude

Gtr. 3 tacet

Rhy. Fig. 3

D5

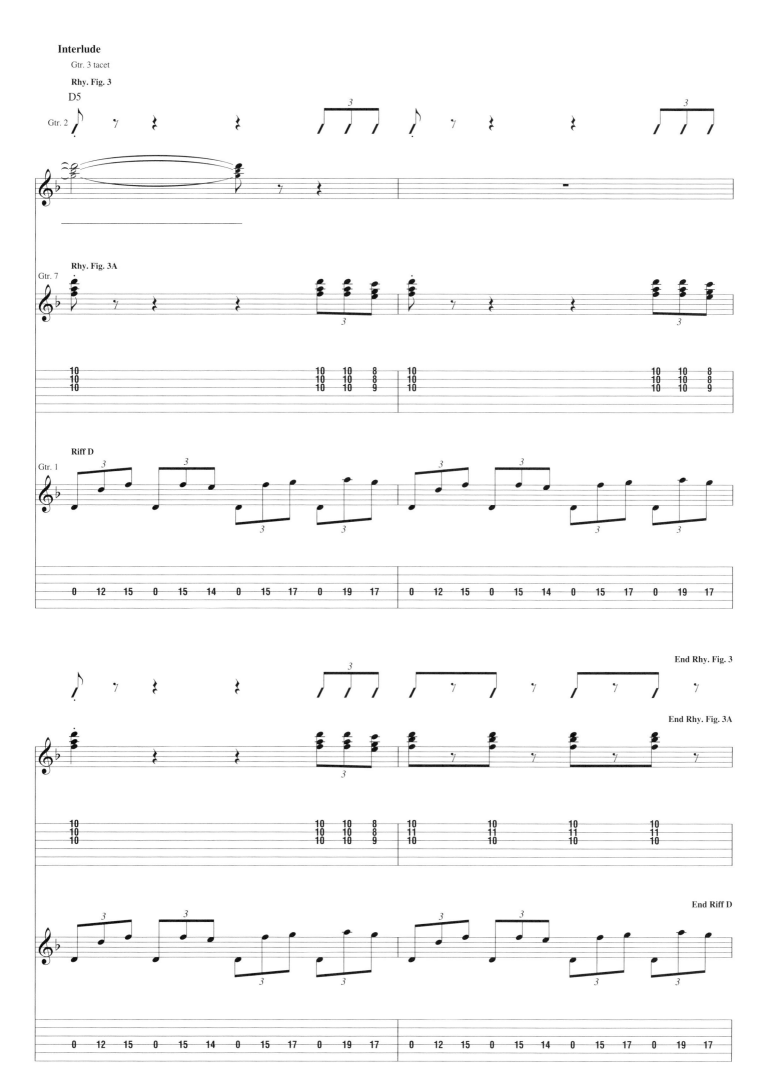

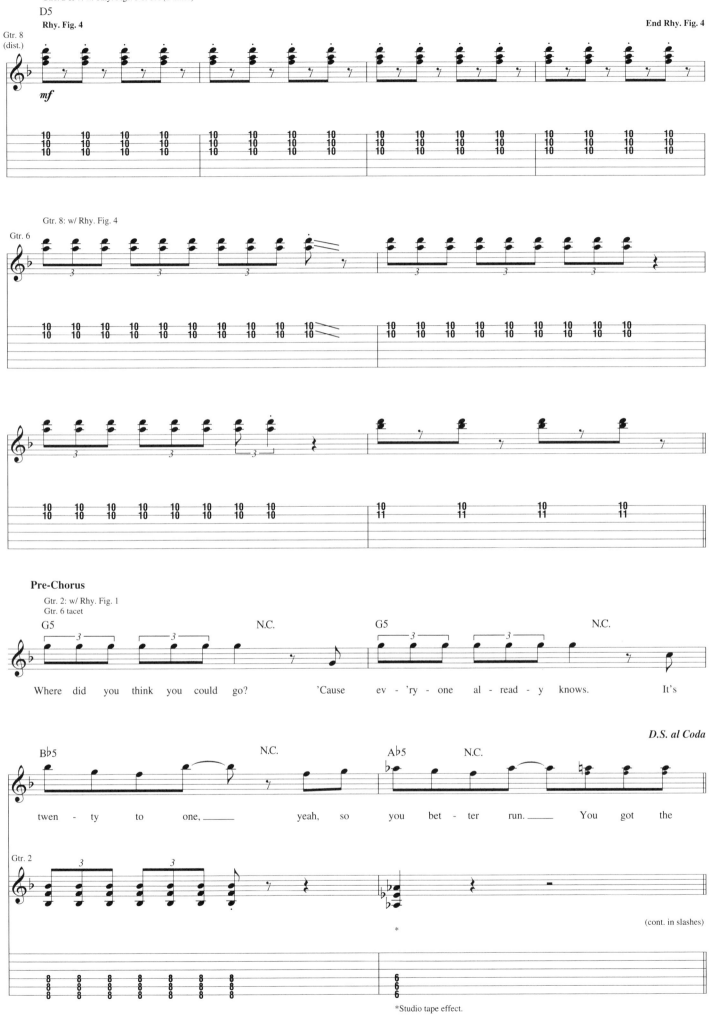

Coda

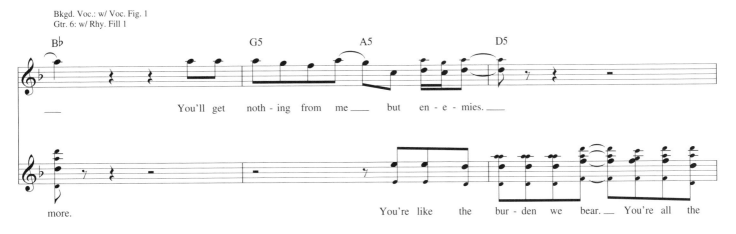

Outro

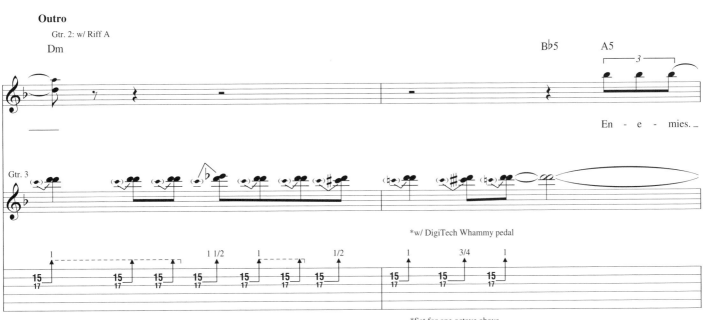

*w/ DigiTech Whammy pedal

*Set for one octave above.

En - e - mies.

Whammy pedal off

I'm Not Alright

Words and Music by Brent Smith, Kathy Sommer, Dana Calitri and Nina Ossoff

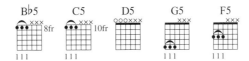

Tuning:
(low to high) D-A-D-A-A-D

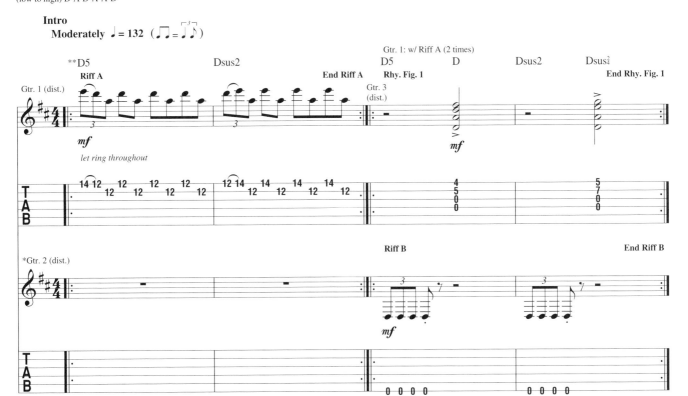

*Doubled throughout

**Chord symbols reflect overall harmony.

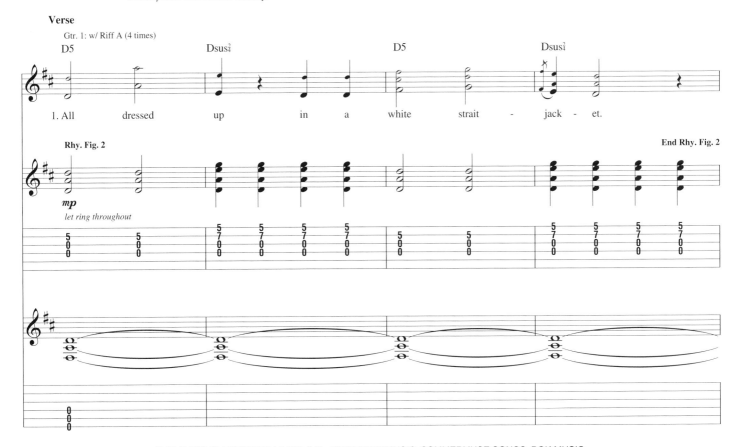

*Played as even eighth-notes.

Bridge

*See top of first page of song for chord diagrams pertaining to rhythm slashes.

D.S. al Coda 2

Gtr. 3 tacet

(cont. in notation)

Whoa, _____ don't care if you a - pol - o - gize. ___ I

___ can't lie. ___ Whoa, _____ I ___ can't lie. __

___ I like to

Gtr. 4

*w/ slide

mf

steady gliss.

56

*Studio pitch shift arranged for gtr.

⊕ Coda 2

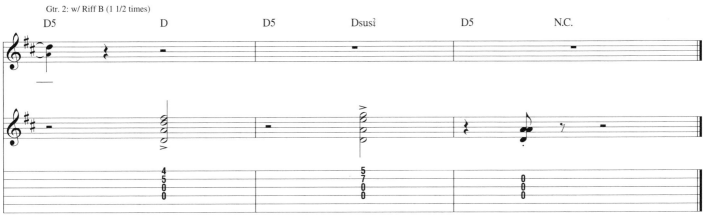

Nowhere Kids

Words and Music by Brent Smith, Dave Bassett and Eric Bass

Drop D tuning, down 1/2 step:
(low to high) Db-Ab-Db-Gb-Bb-Eb

*Chord symbols reflect implied harmony.

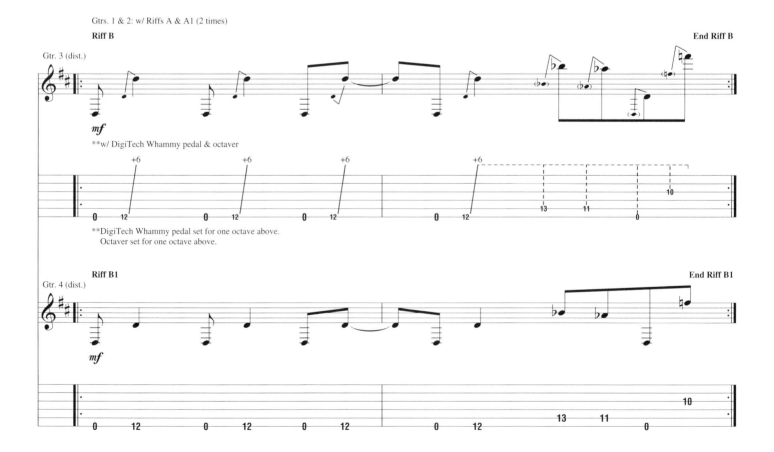

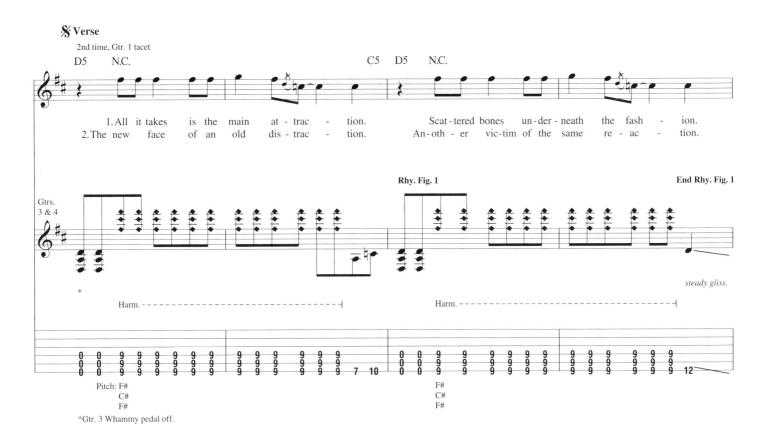

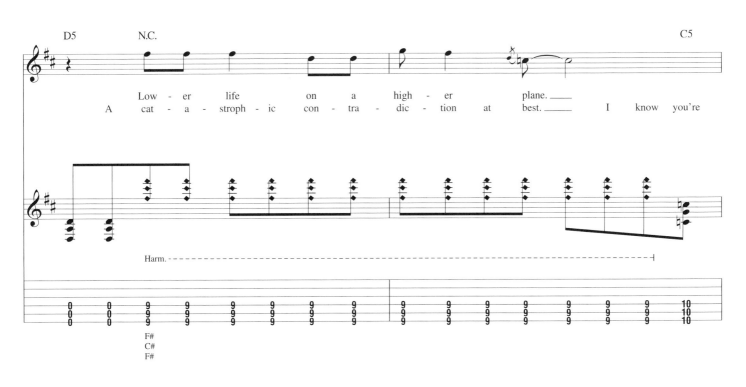

Pre-Chorus

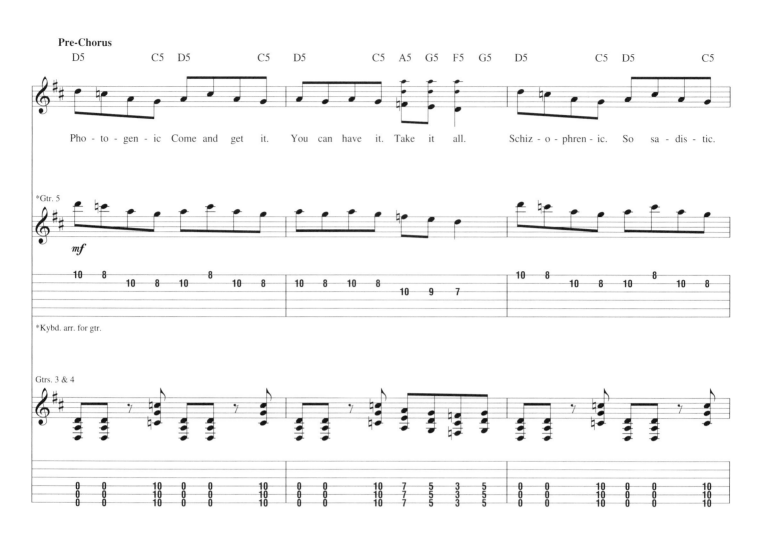

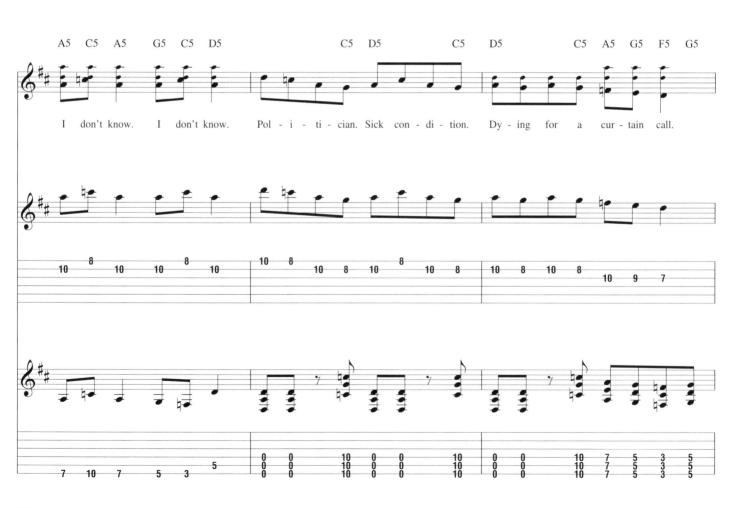

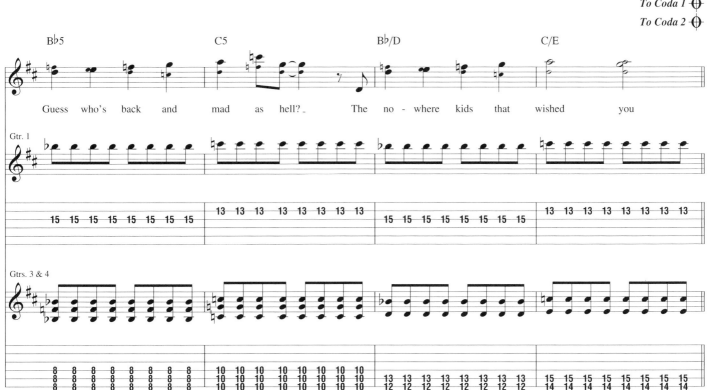
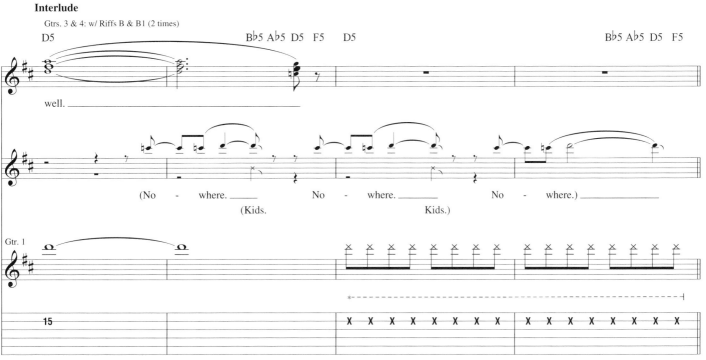

*Tap string with edge of pick.

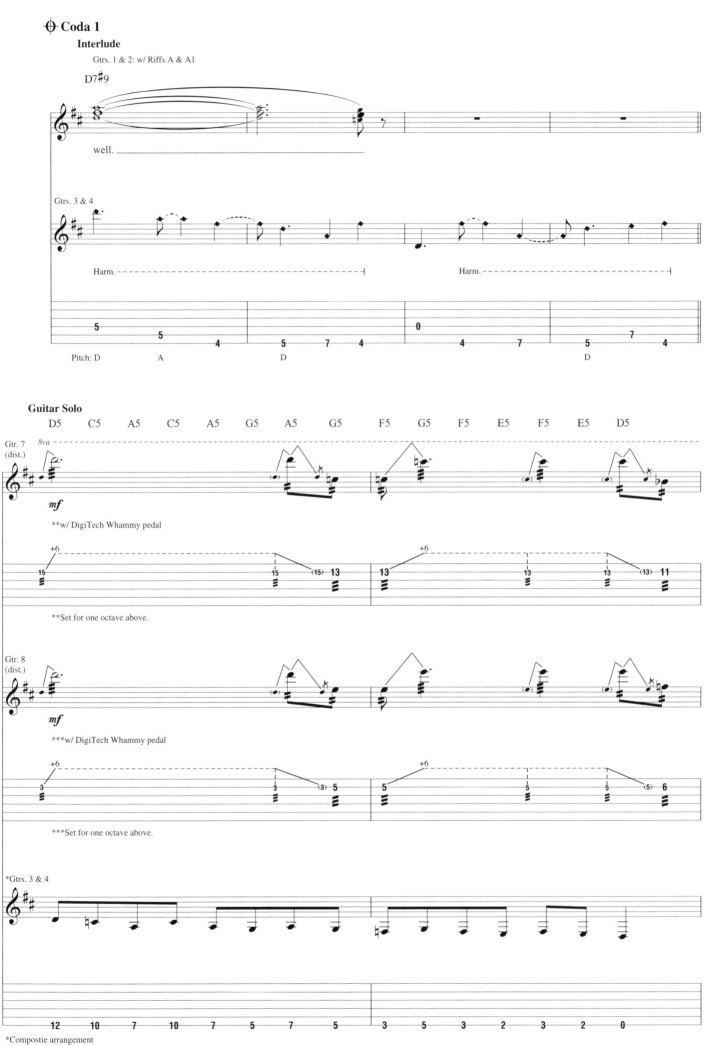

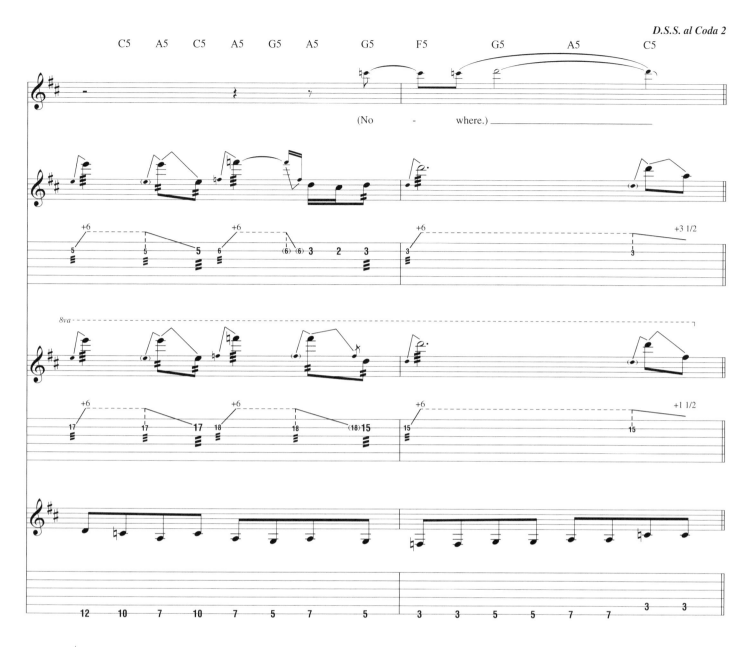

Coda 2

Interlude

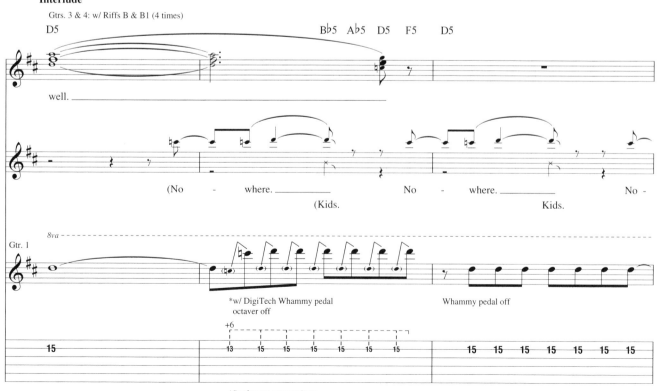

*Set for one octave above.

Miracle

Words and Music by Brent Smith and Dave Bassett

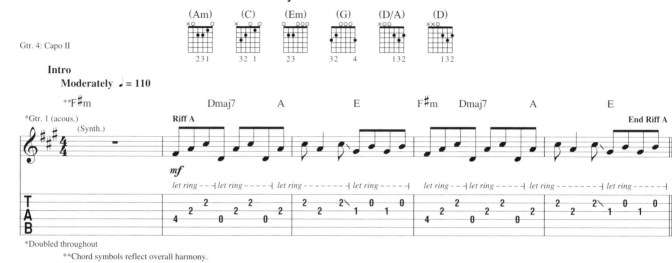

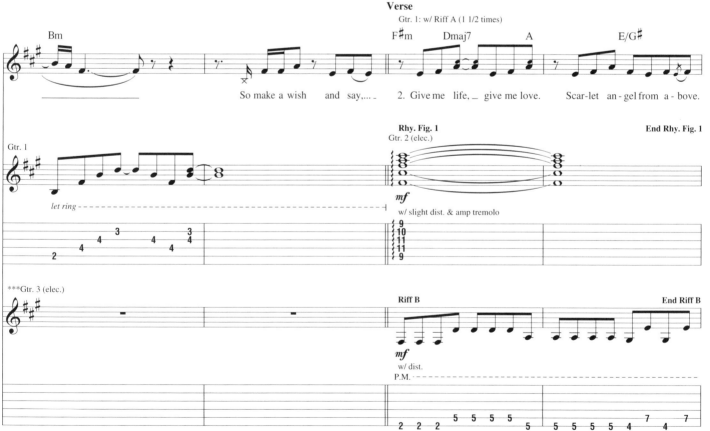

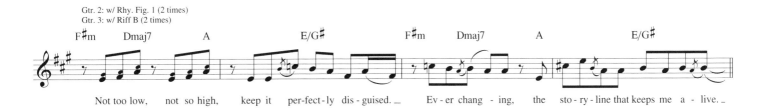

Gtr. 2: w/ Rhy. Fig. 1 (2 times)
Gtr. 3: w/ Riff B (2 times)

F#m   Dmaj7   A   E/G#   F#m   Dmaj7   A   E/G#

Not too low, not so high, keep it per-fect-ly dis-guised. __ Ev-er chang-ing, the sto-ry-line that keeps me a - live. __

Pre-Chorus

Gtrs. 1 & 2 tacet

**(Am)   (C)

*Gtr. 4
(acous.)

mf

_____   My Mo-na Li-sa's mak-in' me smile _____   right be-fore my eyes. __   Take __

Gtr. 2   Gtr. 5 (elec.)

                                                          mf
                                                          w/ dist.

Riff C   **End Riff C**

Gtr. 1

let ring -

Gtr. 3

P.M. -

*Doubled throughout
**Symbols in parentheses represent chord names respective to capoed guitar.
See top of first page of song for chord diagrams pertaining to rhythm slashes.

3rd time, Lead Voc.: w/ Voc. Fill 1
3rd time, Gtr. 7 tacet

an-oth-er look, take a look a-round. It's you and me, it's here and now. As you spar-

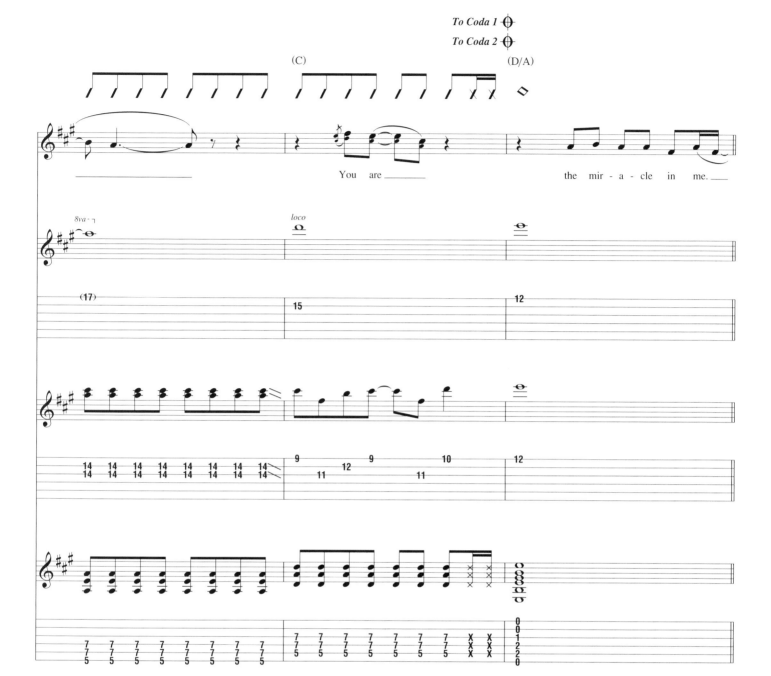

You are _____ the mir - a - cle in me. _____

Interlude
Gtr. 1: w/ Riff A
Gtrs. 3-6 tacet

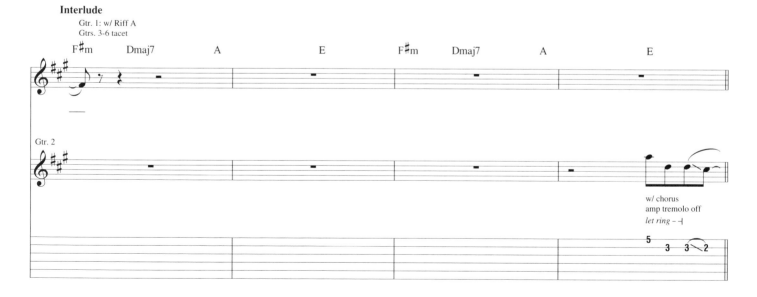

Verse

Gtr. 1: w/ Riff A (1 1/2 times)
Gtr. 3: w/ Riff B (3 times)

3. Show me faith like you do. I'm a-mazed at how you move. ___ Side to side, ___ front to back,

you know how to make it last. ___ Ev-er chang-ing the sto-ry-line that keeps us a-live. ___

D.S. al Coda 1

Pre-Chorus

Gtr. 1: w/ Riff C

Gtr. 2 tacet

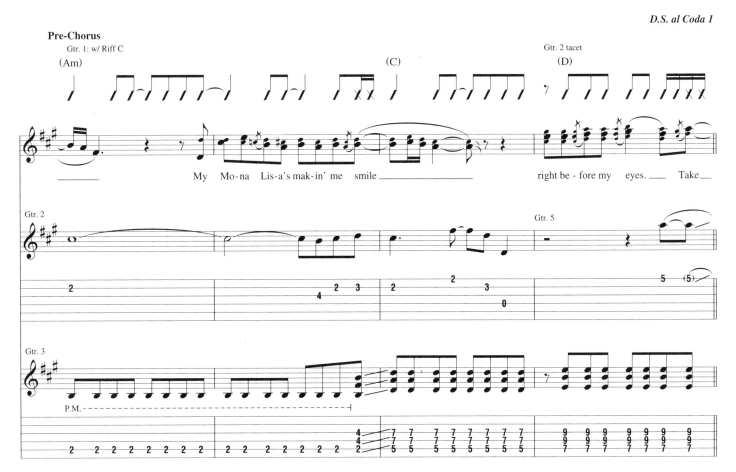

My Mo-na Lis-a's mak-in' me smile ___ right be-fore my eyes. ___ Take ___

⊕ Coda 1

Interlude
Gtrs. 5 & 6 tacet

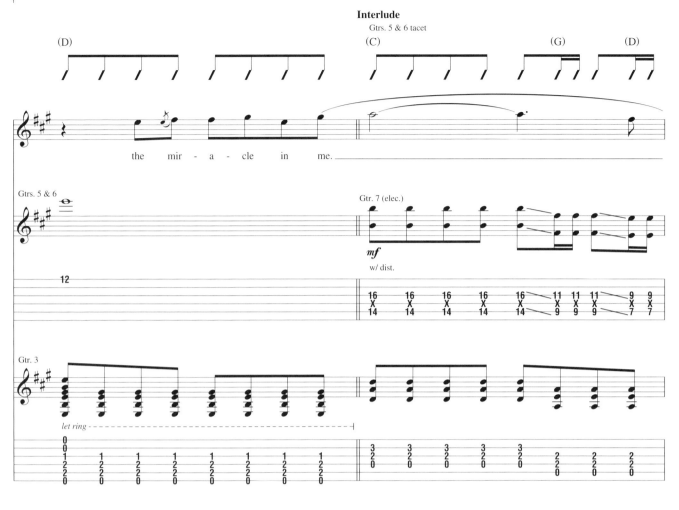

the mir - a - cle in me. _____

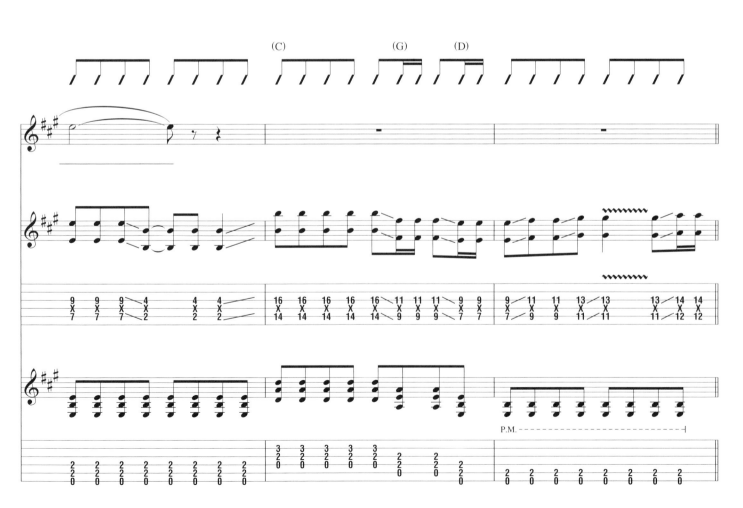

Coda 2

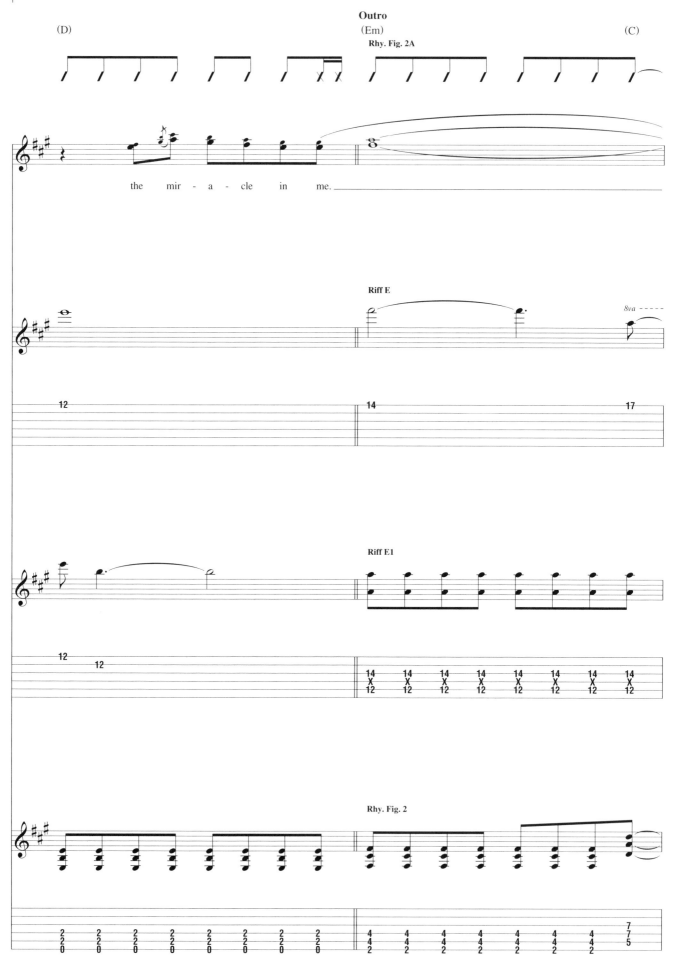

the mir - a - cle in me. _____

76

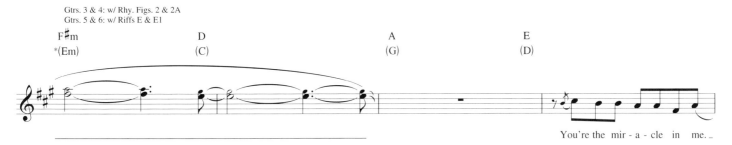

Gtrs. 3 & 4: w/ Rhy. Figs. 2 & 2A
Gtrs. 5 & 6: w/ Riffs E & E1

F#m   D   A   E
*(Em)   (C)   (G)   (D)

You're the mir - a - cle in me.

*Symbols in parentheses represent chord names respective to capoed guitar.
 Symbols above represent actual sounding chords.

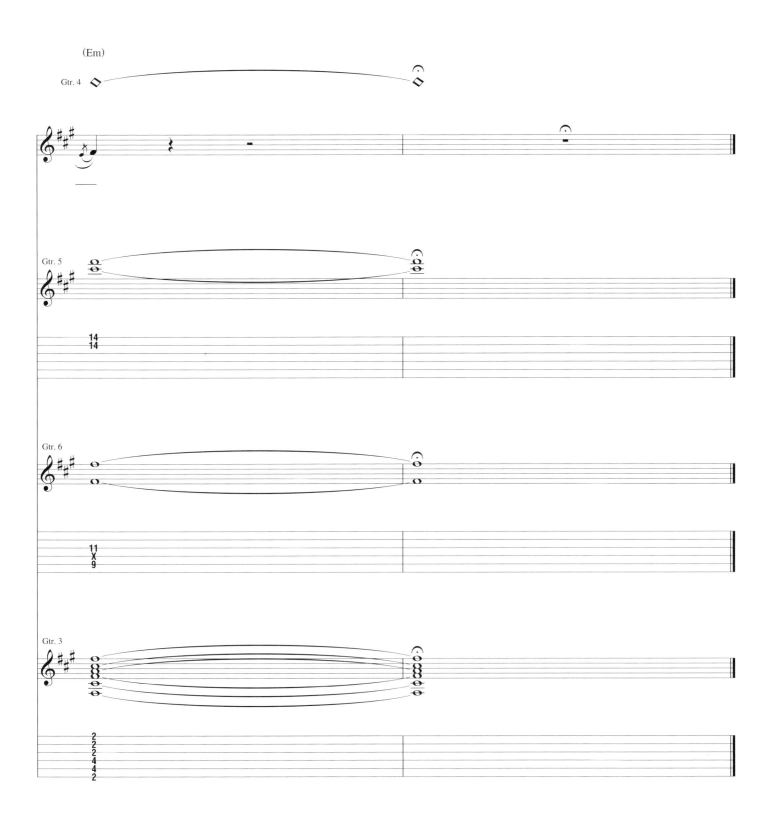

I'll Follow You

Words and Music by Brent Smith, Dave Bassett and Eric Bass

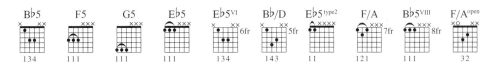

Drop D tuning:
(low to high) D-A-D-G-B-E

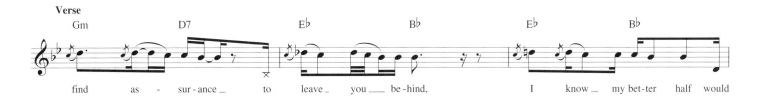

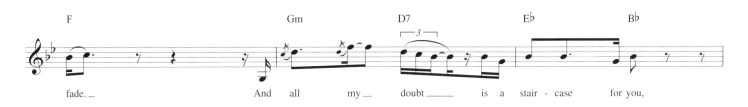

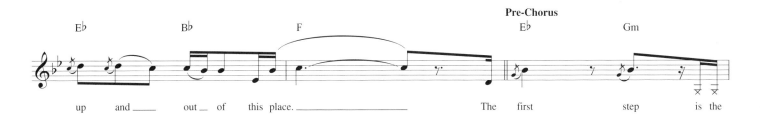

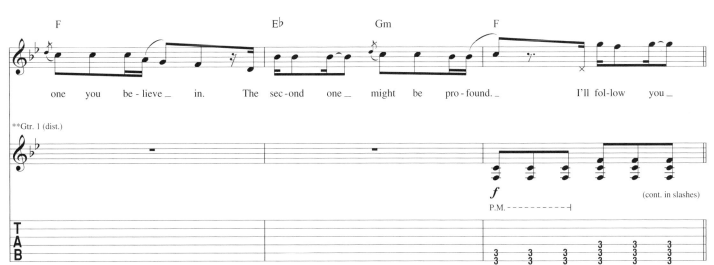

**Doubled throughout

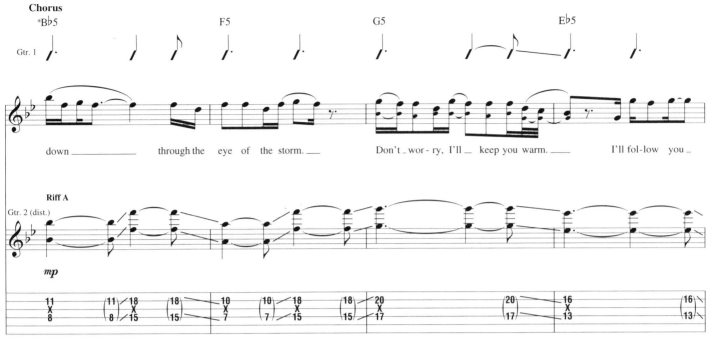

*See top of first page of song for chord diagrams pertaining to rhythm slashes.

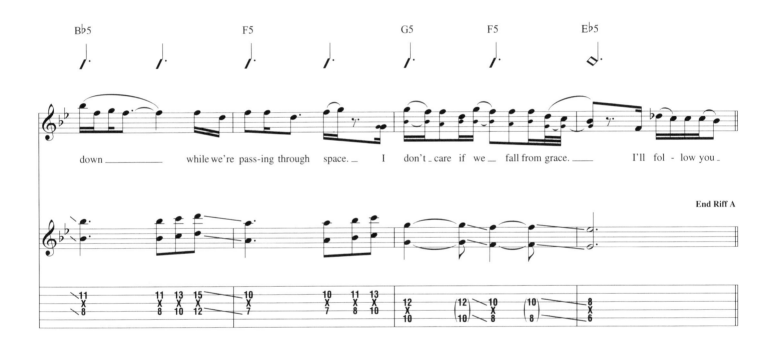

Chorus

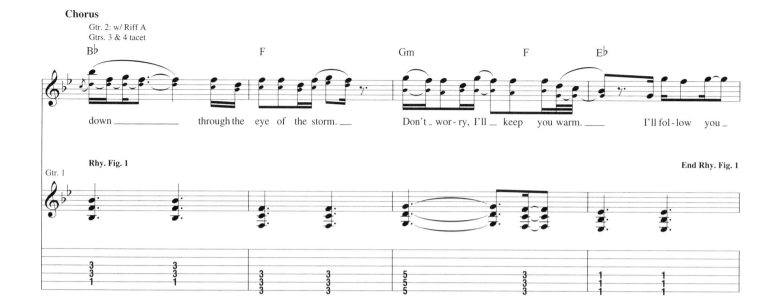

Gtr. 2: w/ Riff A
Gtrs. 3 & 4 tacet

down _____ through the eye of the storm. ___ Don't _ wor - ry, I'll _ keep you warm. ___ I'll fol - low you _

Rhy. Fig. 1   End Rhy. Fig. 1

Gtr. 1

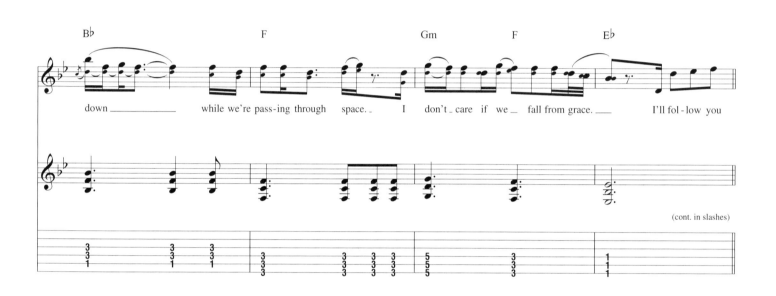

down _____ while we're pass-ing through space. _ I don't _ care if we _ fall from grace. ___ I'll fol - low you

(cont. in slashes)

Bridge

Gtr. 1

down to where for-ev - er lies. With-out a doubt I'm on your side. There's no - where else that I would rath - er

Gtr. 2

82

be. _____ I'm not a-bout to com-pro-mise, give you up to say good-bye. I'll

guide you through the deep. _____ I'll keep you close to me. _____

Guitar Solo

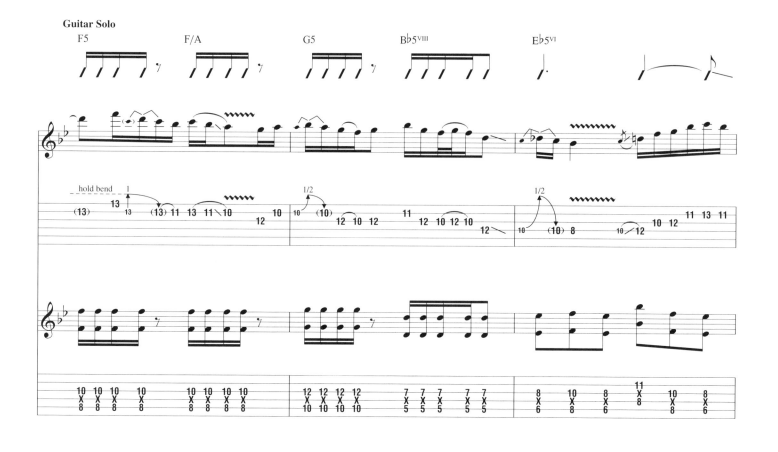

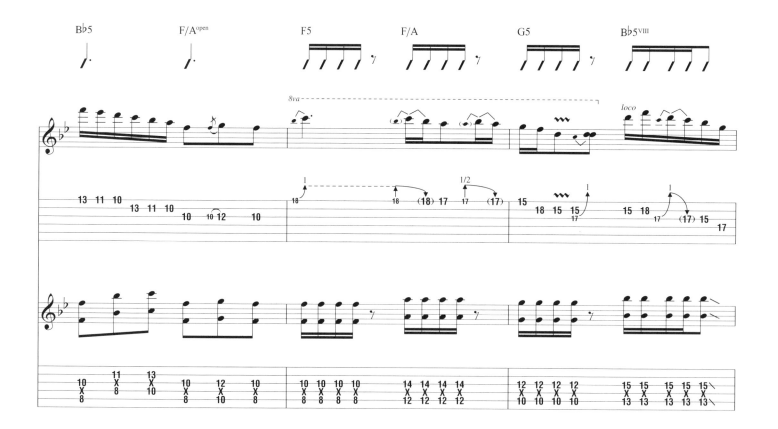

84

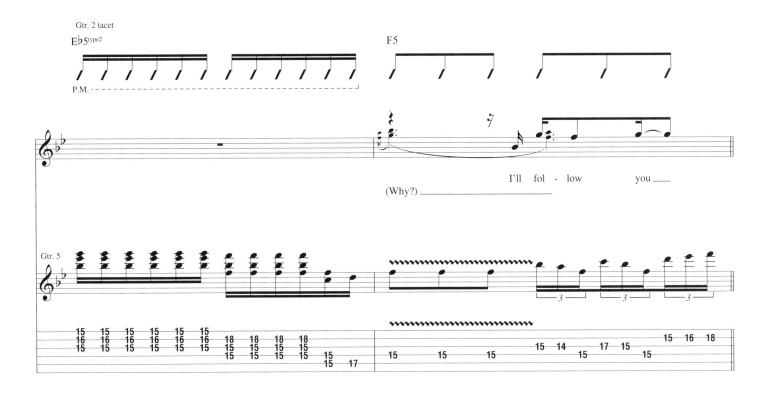

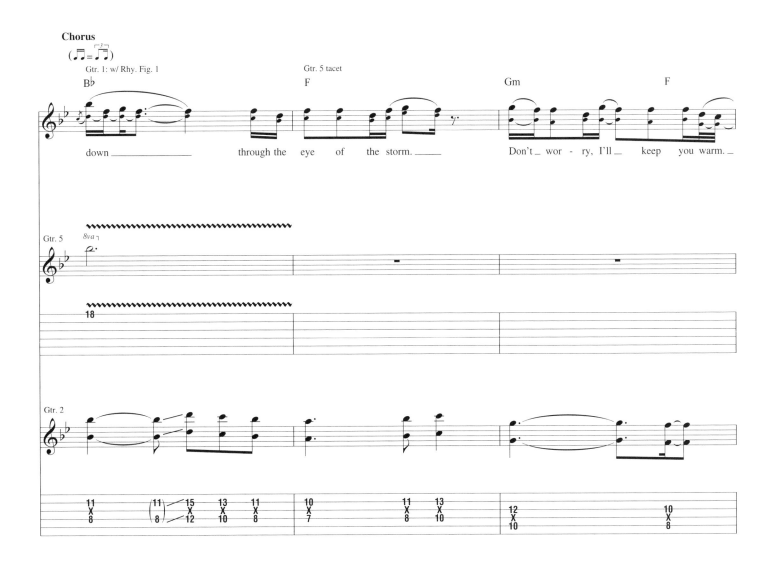

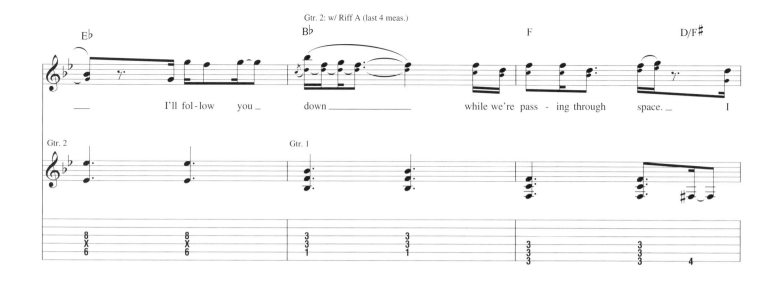

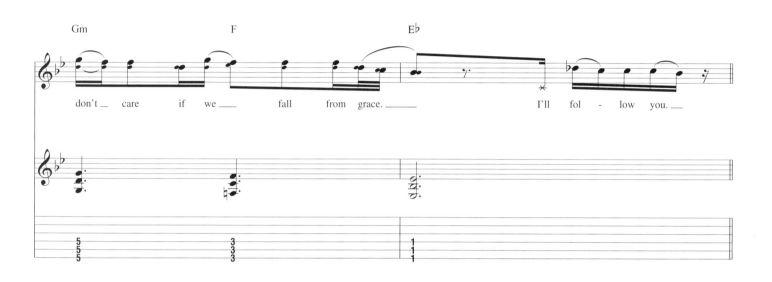

Interlude

Outro-Verse

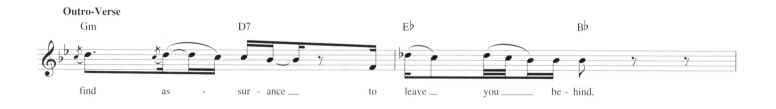

For My Sake

Words and Music by Brent Smith and Dave Bassett

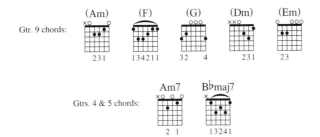

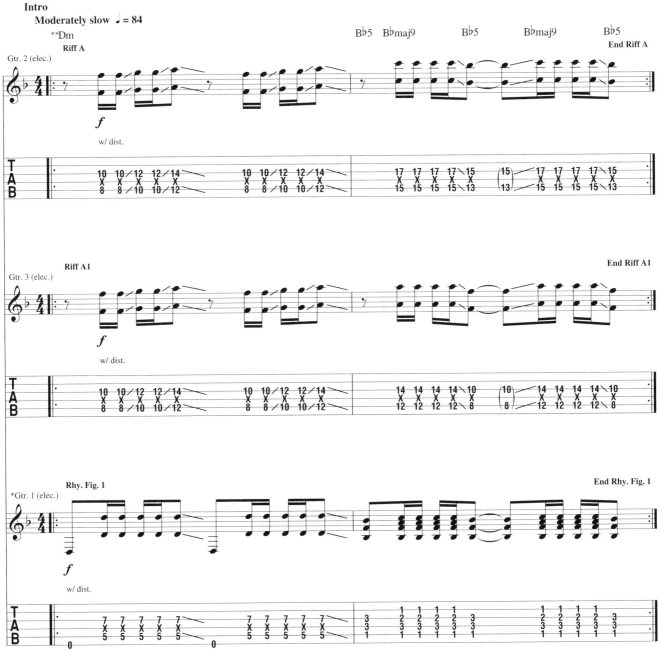

*Doubled throughout

**Chord symbols reflect overall harmony.

Verse

Gtrs. 1, 2 & 3 tacet

1. I re-mem-ber like yes - ter-day,_ you had a dream _ in your eyes and a smile _ on your face and I'm

miss-in' those days a - gain. _ Yeah, I'm miss-in' those days a - gain. _

Gtr. 4: w/ Riff B
Gtr. 5: w/ Riff C (1st 2 meas.)

And I for-got what real - ly got in the way._ May-be the sun that would-n't shine should be tak - in' the blame. _ 'Cause it's

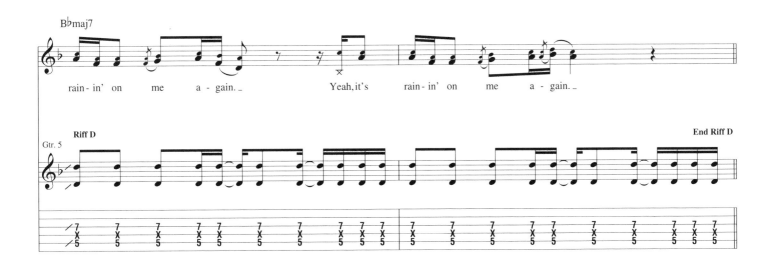

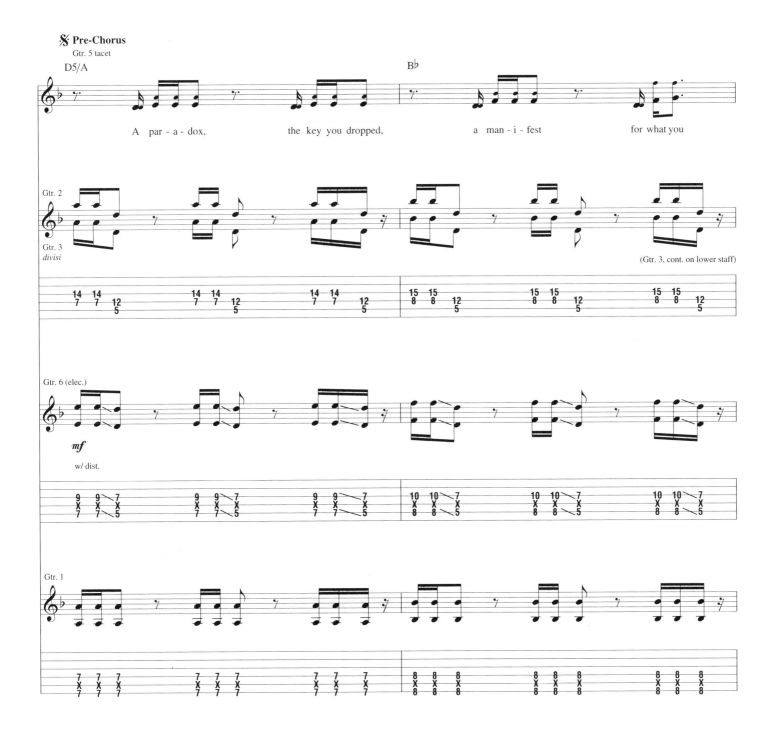

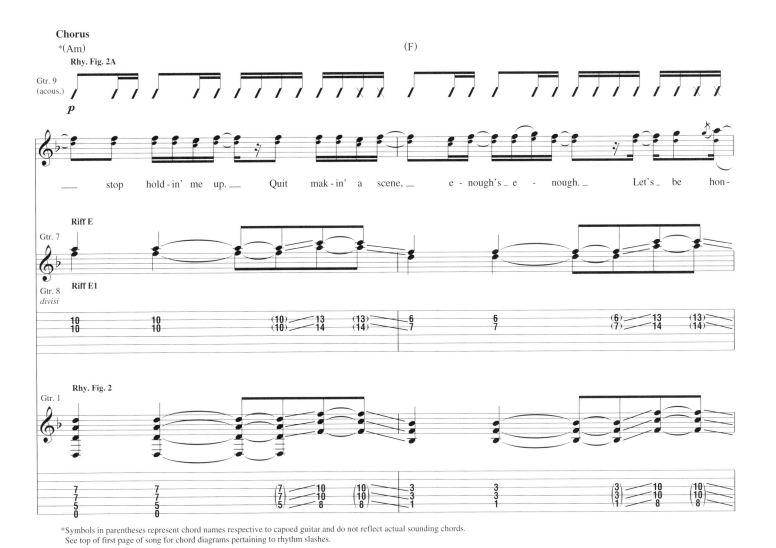

*Symbols in parentheses represent chord names respective to capoed guitar and do not reflect actual sounding chords.
See top of first page of song for chord diagrams pertaining to rhythm slashes.

Gtrs. 1 & 9: w/ Rhy. Figs. 2 & 2A
Gtrs. 7 & 8: w/ Riffs E & E1

Dm
*(Am)

Bb
(F)

___ I'm call-in' you out. There's noth-in' left ___ for us ___ here ___ now. ___ Let's ___ be hon-

*Symbols in parentheses represent chord names respective to capoed guitar.
Symbols above represent actual sounding chords.

To Coda ⊕

C
(G)

Gm
(Dm)

Am
(Em)

Bb
(F)

C
(G)

-est, I prom-ise I'm nev-er look-in' back ___ for my ___ sake.

Interlude

Gtr. 1: w/ Rhy. Fig. 1 (2 times)
Gtrs. 2 & 3: w/ Riffs A & A1 (2 times)

Dm
(Am)

Bb
(F)

For my ___ sake.

Rhy. Fig. 3

Gtr. 9

End Rhy. Fig. 3

**Capoed fret is "0" in tab.

Gtr. 9: w/ Rhy. Fig. 3

Dm
(Am)

Bb
(F)

Verse

Gtr. 4: w/ Riff B (2 times)
Gtr. 5: w/ Riff C (1 1/2 times)

Dm7

2. Tell me some-thin' that's po-et-ic at best, ___ make me be-lieve there was a time that you were-n't like the rest, and I'll

Riff F

Gtr. 10 (elec.)

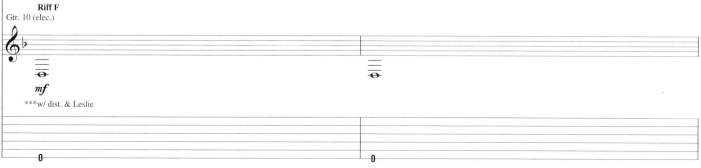

mf

***w/ dist. & Leslie

***Set rotary pulse on Leslie for sixteenth-note regeneration.

92

B♭maj7

nev - er ask you a - gain. ___ And I'll nev - er ask you a - gain. ___

End Riff F

Gtr. 10: w/ Riff F

Dm7

For all the mo-ments and the mem-o - - ries, ___ no one could ev - er say we nev-er had a his - to-ry, but I'm

D.S. al Coda

Gtr. 5: w/ Riff D

B♭maj7

leav - in' that all be - hind. ___ And there's noth-ing gon - na change my mind. ___

Coda

Interlude

Gtr. 1: w/ Rhy. Fig. 1 (2 times)
Gtrs. 2 & 3: w/ Riffs A & A1 (2 times)
Gtr. 9: w/ Rhy. Fig. 3 (2 times)

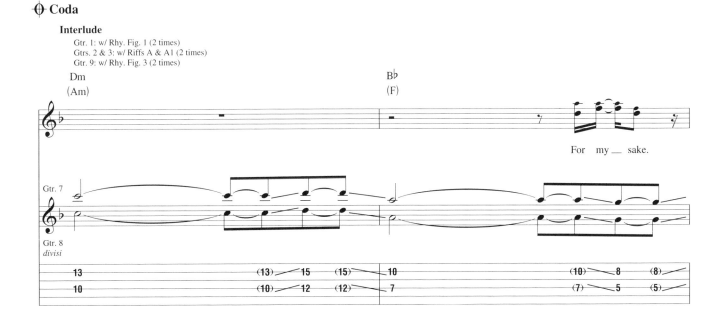

Dm
(Am)

B♭
(F)

For my ___ sake.

Gtr. 7

Gtr. 8
divisi

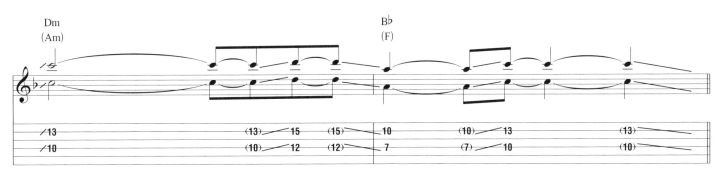

Dm
(Am)

B♭
(F)

Pre-Chorus

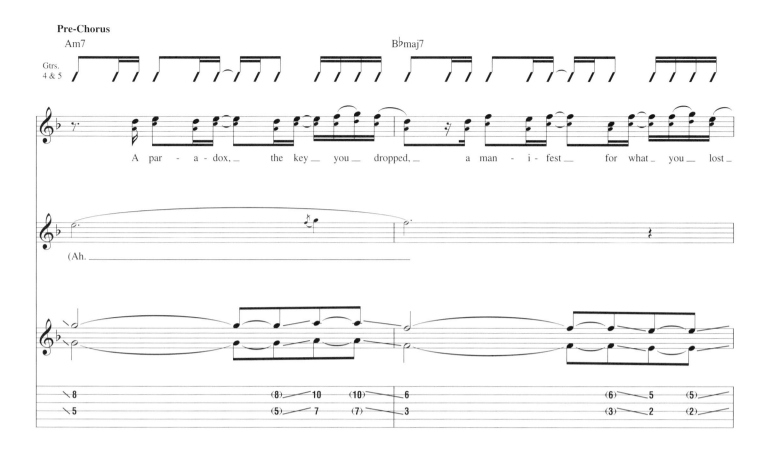

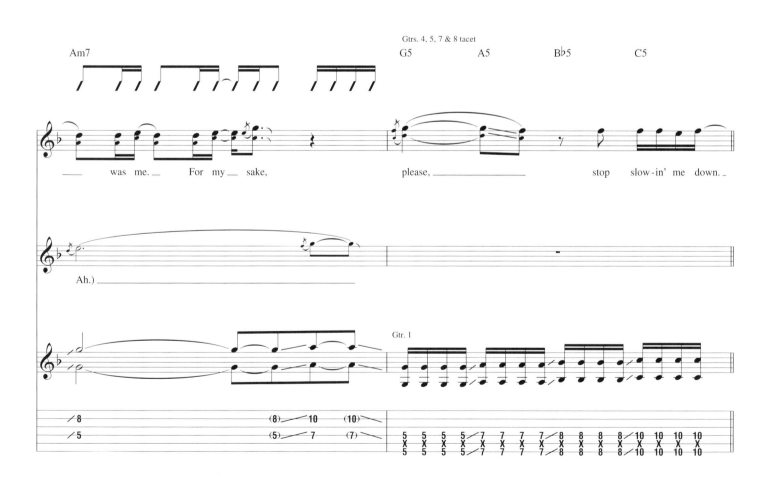

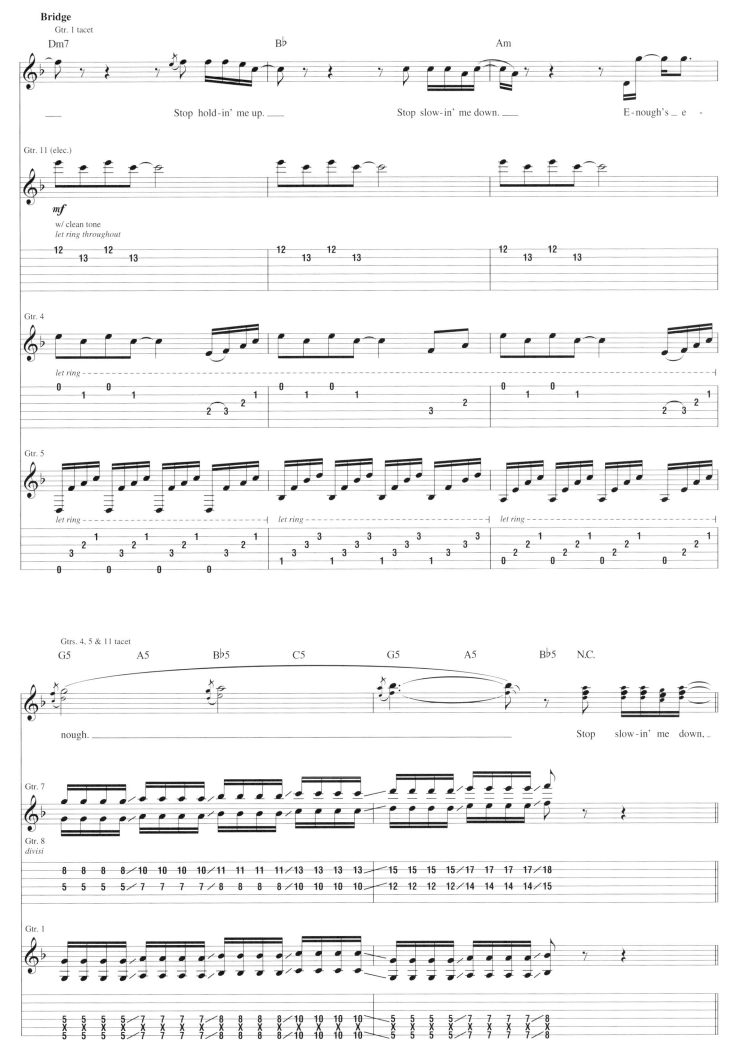

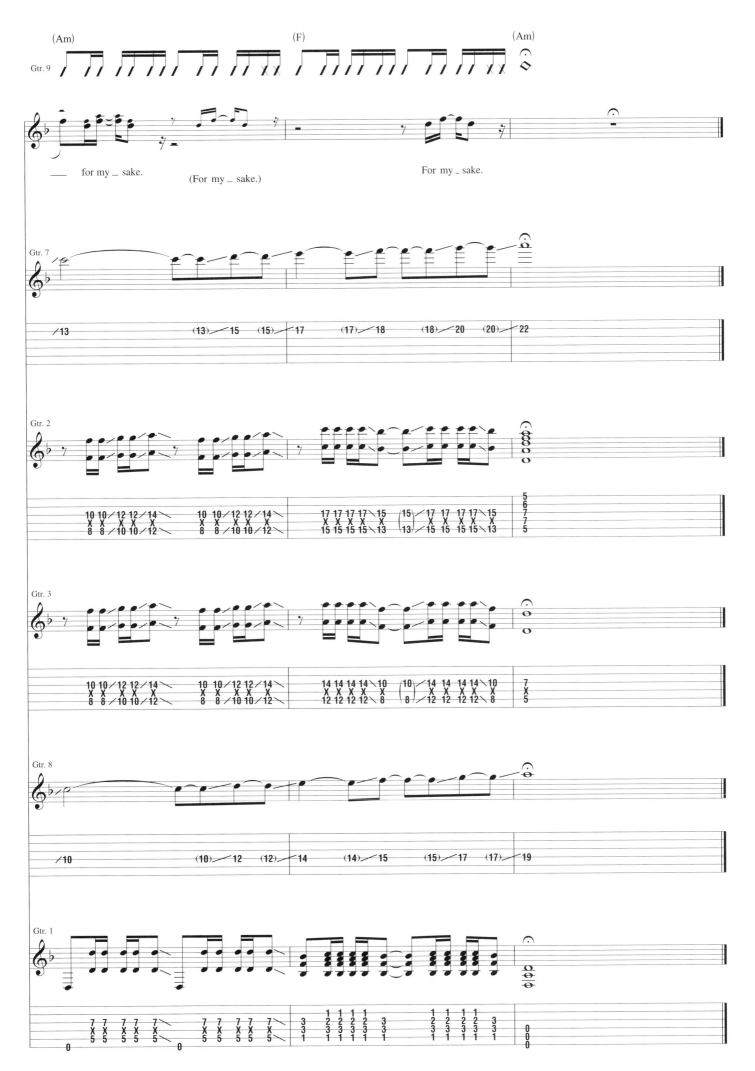

My Name

(Wearing Me Out)

Words and Music by Brent Smith and Dave Bassett

Drop D tuning, down 1 step:
(low to high) C-G-C-F-A-D

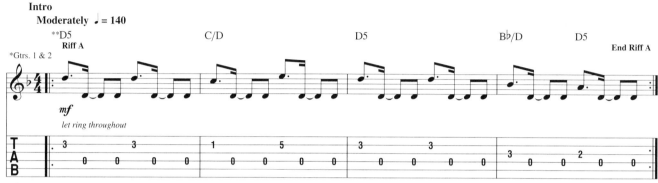

*Gtr. 1 (acous.); Gtr. 2 (elec. sitar) w/ clean tone.

**Chord symbols reflect implied harmony.

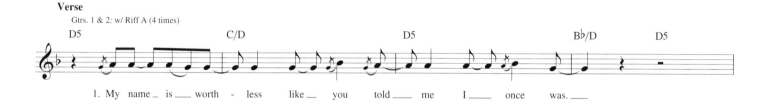

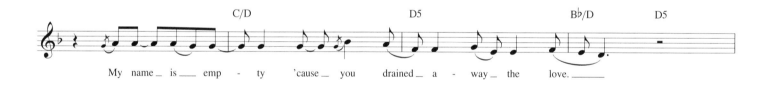

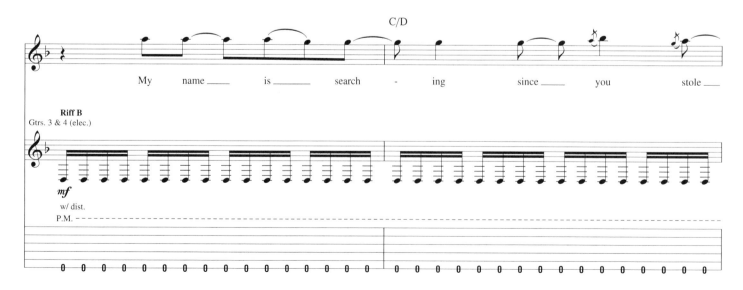

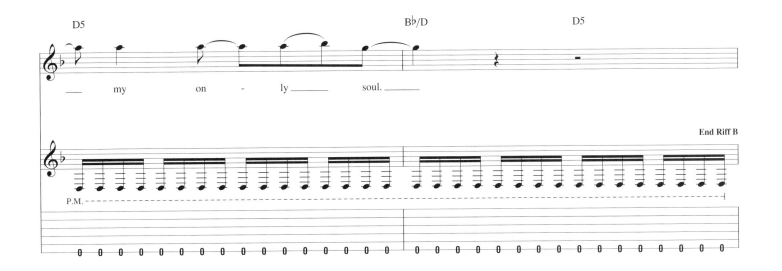

my on - ly soul.

End Riff B

P.M.

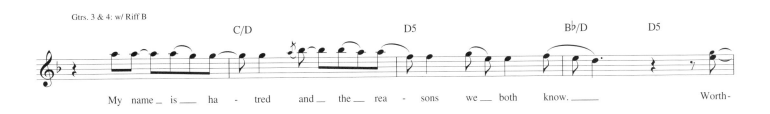

Gtrs. 3 & 4: w/ Riff B

C/D   D5   Bb/D   D5

My name is ha - tred and the rea - sons we both know. _____ Worth-

Bb

- less, emp - ty, search - ing, ha - tred. Well,

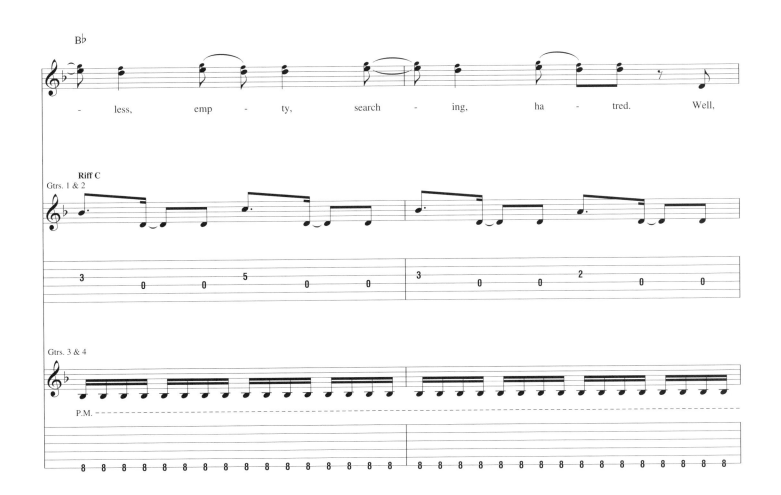

Riff C
Gtrs. 1 & 2

P.M.

Gtrs. 3 & 4

A

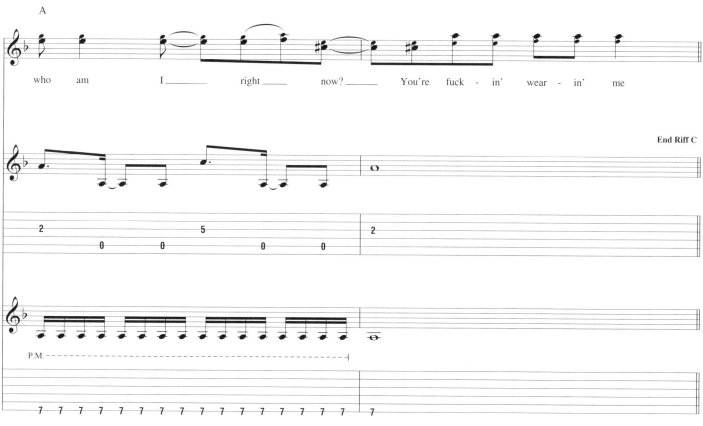

who am I right now? You're fuck - in' wear - in' me

End Riff C

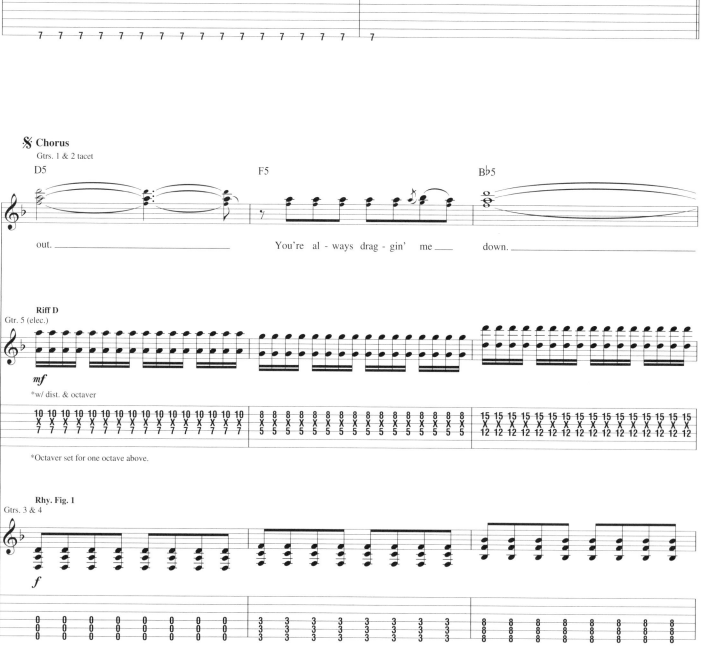

𝄋 Chorus
Gtrs. 1 & 2 tacet

D5   F5   B♭5

out.   You're al - ways drag - gin' me down.

Riff D
Gtr. 5 (elec.)

*w/ dist. & octaver

*Octaver set for one octave above.

Rhy. Fig. 1
Gtrs. 3 & 4

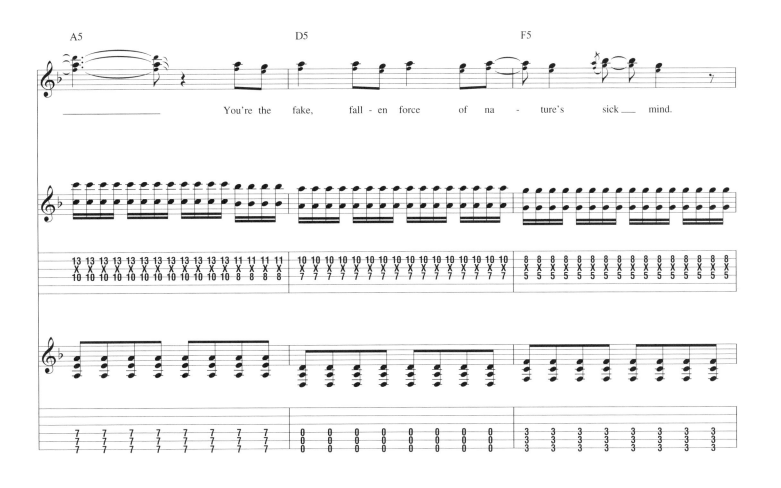

You're the fake, fall-en force of na - ture's sick __ mind.

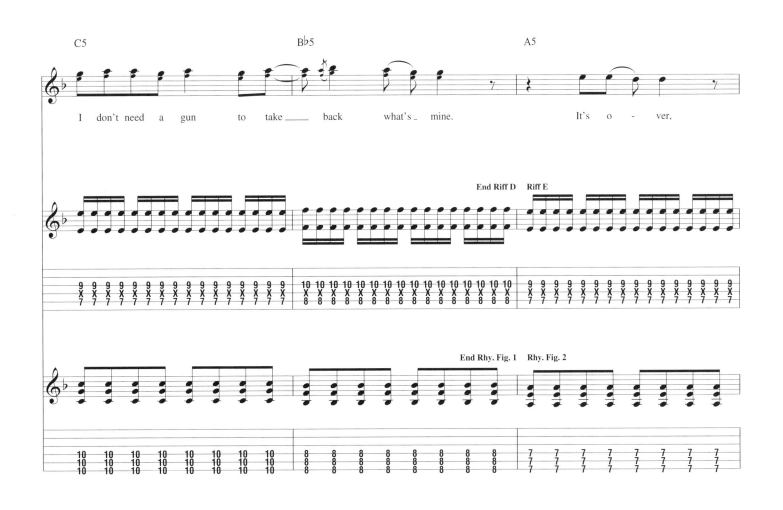

I don't need a gun to take __ back what's __ mine. It's o - ver,

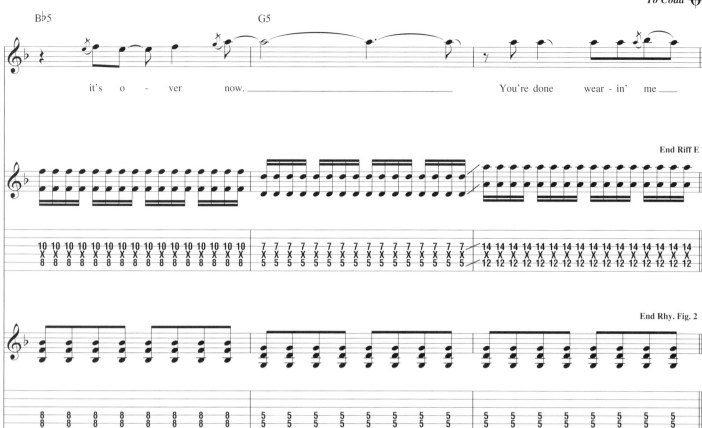

it's o - ver now. _____ You're done wear - in' me _____

Interlude

Gtrs. 1 & 2: w/ Riff A
Gtrs. 3, 4 & 5 tacet

| D5 | C/D | D5 | Bb/D | D5 |

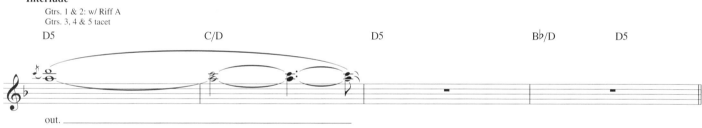

out. _____

Verse

Gtrs. 1 & 2: w/ Riff A (2 times)
Gtrs. 3 & 4: w/ Riff B (2 times)

| D5 | C/D | D5 | Bb/D | D5 |

2. My name _ is scream - ing like _ the sound _ of your _ heart fail - ing.

| C/D | D5 | Bb/D | D5 |

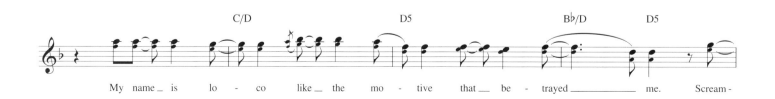

My name _ is lo - co like _ the mo - tive that _ be - trayed _____ me. Scream -

D.S. al Coda

Coda

Bridge

You're wear-in' me out, ___ you're wear-in' me out, ___ you're wear-in' me out. _____

Gtr. 3: w/ Riff F
Gtrs. 4 & 5: w/ Riff F1

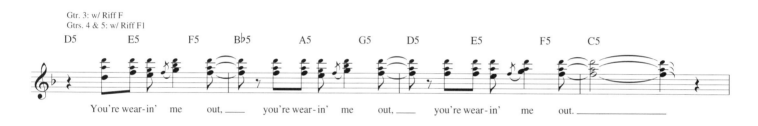

You'll _ be an - cient his - t'ry, but who am I ___ right _ now? _____

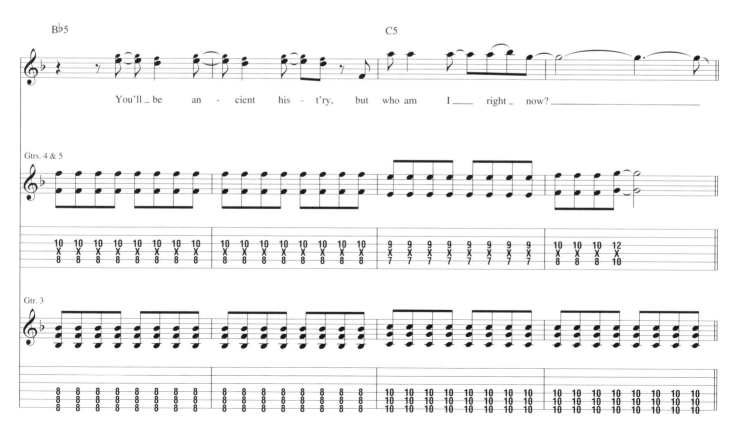

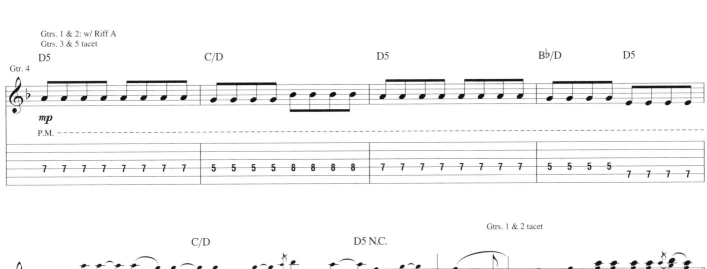

Chorus

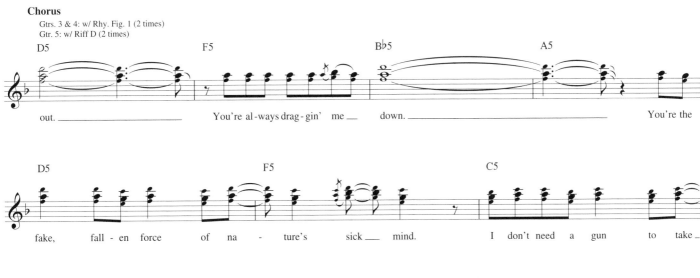

105

fake, fall-en force of na - ture's sick __ mind. I don't need a gun to take __ back what's __ mine.

Gtrs. 3 & 4: w/ Rhy. Fig. 2
Gtr. 5: w/ Riff E

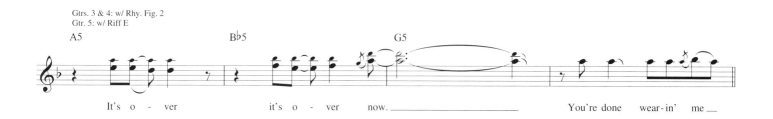

It's o - ver it's o - ver now. _____ You're done wear-in' me __

Outro

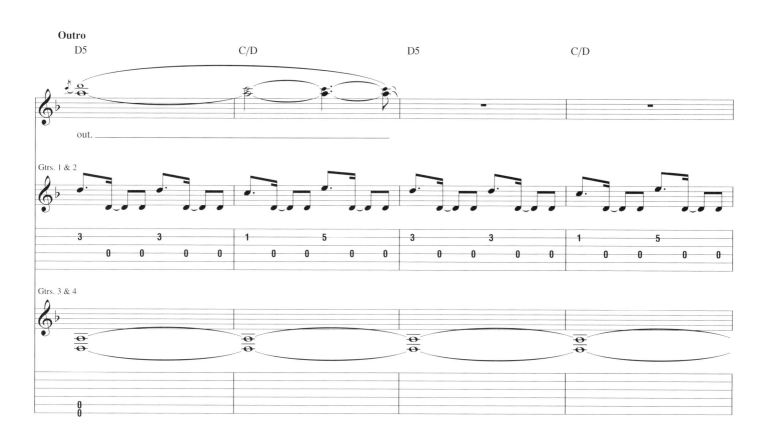

out. _____

Gtrs. 1 & 2

Gtrs. 3 & 4

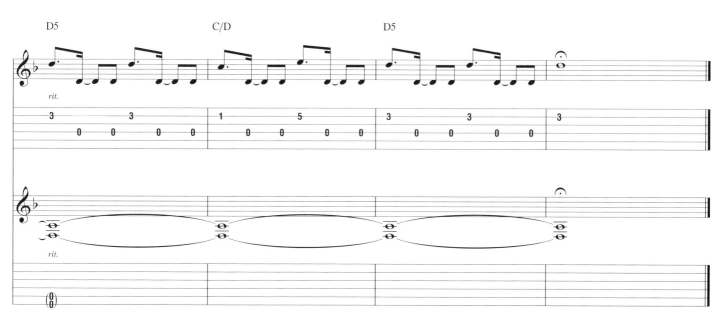

Through the Ghost

Words and Music by Brent Smith and Dave Bassett

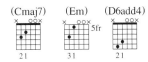

Capo III

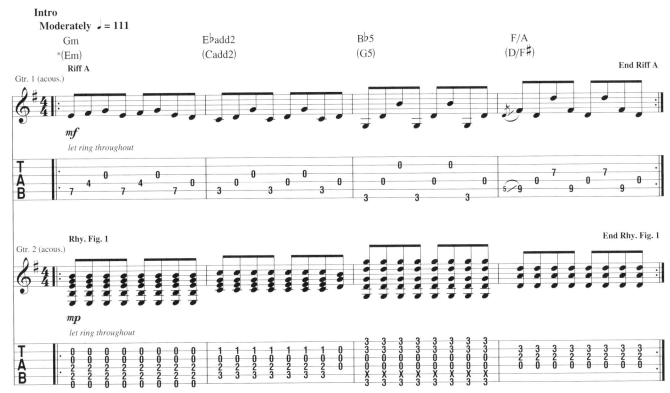

*Symbols in parentheses represent chord names respective to capoed guitar.
Symbols above reflect actual sounding chords. Capoed fret is "0" in tab.
Chord symbols reflect overall harmony.

Verse

Gtr. 1: w/ Riff A (2 times)
Gtr. 2: w/ Rhy. Fig. 1 (2 times)

1. Speak of the dev — il, ___ look ___ who just ___ walked in — to the room, ___
2. So man — y si — lent ___ sor — rows you'll nev — er hear ___ from a — gain. ___

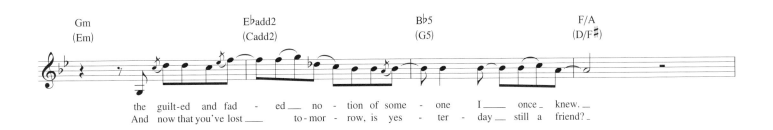

the guilt-ed and fad — ed ___ no — tion of some — one I ___ once ___ knew. ___
And now that you've lost ___ to — mor — row, is yes — ter — day ___ still a friend? ___

*(Cmaj7)   (Em)   (D6add4)

All the per-fect mo-ments are wrong. _
All the bridg-es we built were burned. _

All the pre-cious piec-es are gone. _
Not a sin-gle les-son was learned. _

*See top of first page of song for chord diagrams pertaining to rhythm slashes.

Gtr. 1: w/ Riff B
Gtr. 2: w/ Rhy. Fig. 2

E♭maj7   Gm   F6add4
(Cmaj7)   (Em)   (D6add4)

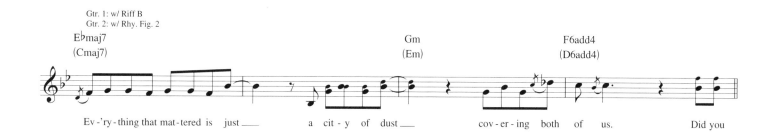

Ev-'ry-thing that mat-tered is just _ a cit-y of dust _ cov-er-ing both of us. Did you

Chorus

E♭add9 B♭5 Gm   E♭add9 B♭5 Gm
(Cadd9) (G5) (Em)   (Cadd9) (G5) (Em)

hide your-self _ a-way? _ I can't see you an - y-more. _ Did you e-

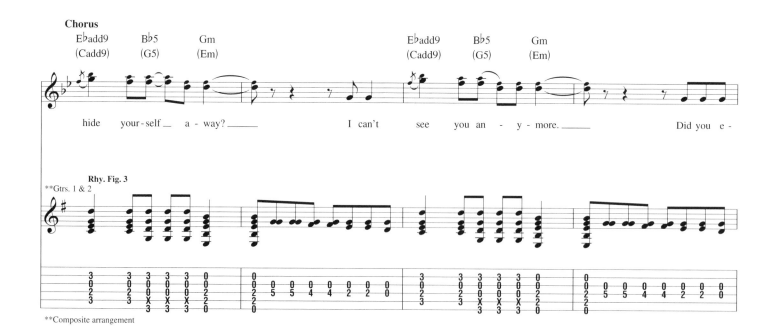

Rhy. Fig. 3
**Gtrs. 1 & 2

**Composite arrangement

108

Coda

E♭maj7
(Cmaj7)

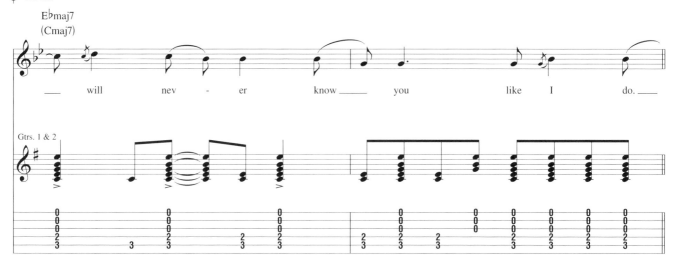

___ will nev - er know ____ you like I do. ____

Bridge

E♭maj7   Gm   Fadd4
(Cmaj7)   (Em)   (Dadd4)

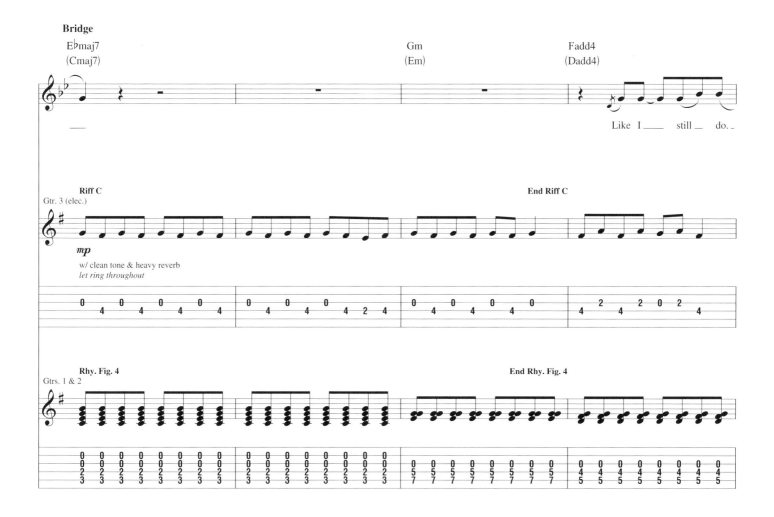

___   Like I ___ still ___ do. ___

Gtrs. 1 & 2: w/ Rhy. Fig. 4
Gtr. 3: w/ Riff C

E♭maj7   Gm
(Cmaj7)   (Em)

___

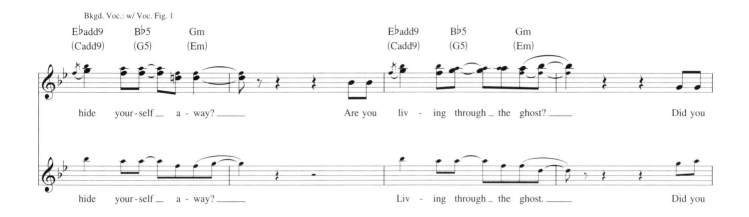

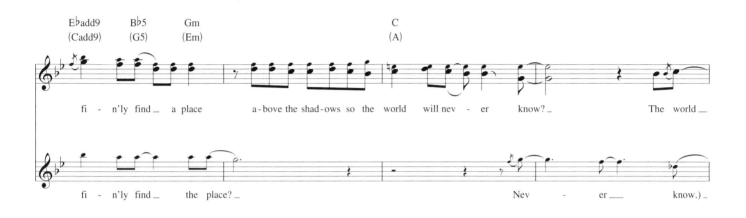

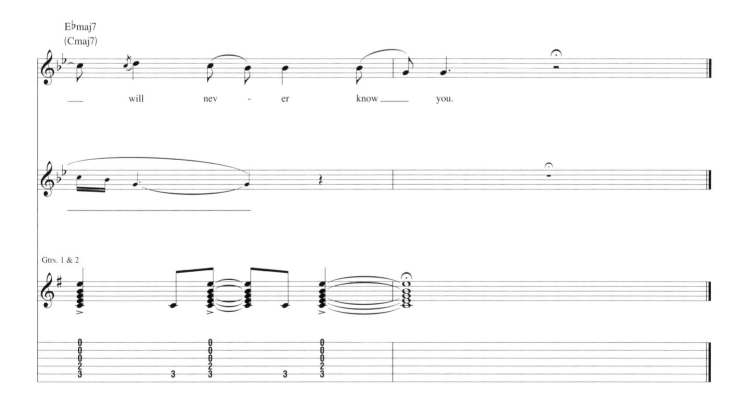